P9-DFQ-917

Conquering C++ Pointers

Conquering C++ Pointers

Robert J. Traister
Robert J. Traister & Associates
Front Royal, Virginia

ACADEMIC PRESS PROFESSIONAL, INC.
Harcourt Brace & Company, Publishers

Boston   San Diego   New York
London   Sydney   Tokyo   Toronto

This book is printed on acid-free paper ⊗

Copyright © 1994 by Academic Press, Inc.
All rights reserved
No part of this publication may be reproduced or transmitted in any form
or by any means, electronic or mechanical, including photocopy,
recording, or any information storage and retrieval system, without
permission in writing from the publisher.

AP PROFESSIONAL
955 Massachusetts Avenue, Cambridge, MA 02139

An Imprint of ACADEMIC PRESS, INC.
A Division of HARCOURT BRACE & COMPANY

United Kingdom Edition published by
ACADEMIC PRESS LIMITED
24-28 Oval Road, London NW1 7DX

Library of Congress Cataloging-in-Publication Data

Traister, Robert J.
    Conquering C++ pointers / Robert J. Traister
      p.   cm.
    Includes index.
    ISBN 0-12-697420-9
    1. C++ (Computer program language) I. Title.
    QA76.73.C153T733   1993
    005.13'3—dc20   93-23739
                                         CIP

Printed in the United States of America
94 95 96 97 EB 9 8 7 6 5 4 3 2 1

For Jack and Peggy Ellis

About the Author

Robert J. Traister is a professional writer and programmer who has authored 115 technical books. It is believed that he has written more books about C and C++ programming than any other author, and his texts have been translated into French, German, Japanese, Italian, Arabic, Korean, Portuguese, Spanish, and Russian.

He currently lectures on C++ to college audiences and conducts seminars on this subject for the Federal government and private industry.

Mr. Traister resides in the foothills of Northwestern Virginia.

Contents

Preface

Conquering C++ Pointers is a book about the entire C++ language, because pointers address everything that makes up this language. If you don't fully understand pointers, their uses, and their capabilities, then you don't understand C++. Anything that takes place within this language utilizes pointers, often invisibly.

Pointers have been characterized by many as the bogeyman of the student learning C++. Books about C++ typically only mention pointers in an insignificant chapter. A single chapter is not enough, however, because pointers are an integral part of the entire language. *Conquering C++ Pointers* discusses the ways C++ pointers interact or can be made to interact with other program elements.

The reader will quickly realize that pointers are just variables and bear similarities to all other variables. However, pointers are *special* variables since they store memory addresses and allow access to objects at these addresses. Accessing objects via pointers is often a more efficient method of addressing many tasks. In some situations, pointer operations may be the only means of accomplishing a goal.

The purpose of this book is to unmask pointers for what they are. The reader will quickly accept pointers as another type of variable that is a powerful part of the versatile C++ took kit. Indeed, the pointer is the true power behind C++ programs, and by mastering its many operations, the C++ programmer will be able ot harness all of this power and direct it toward a more efficient means of problem solving.

LIMITED WARRANTY AND DISCLAIMER OF LIABILITY

ACADEMIC PRESS, INC. ("AP") AND ANYONE ELSE WHO HAS BEEN INVOLVED IN THE CREATION OR PRODUCTION OF THE ACCOMPANYING CODE ("THE PRODUCT") CANNOT AND DO NOT WARRANT THE PERFORMANCE OR RESULTS THAT MAY BE OBTAINED BY USING THE PRODUCT. THE PRODUCT IS SOLD "AS IS" WITHOUT WARRANTY OF ANY KIND (EXCEPT AS HEREAFTER DESCRIBED), EITHER EXPRESSED OR IMPLIED, INCLUDING, BUT NOT LIMITED TO, ANY WARRANTY OF PERFORMANCE OR ANY IMPLIED WARRANTY OF MERCHANTABILITY OR FITNESS FOR ANY PARTICULAR PURPOSE. AP WARRANTS ONLY THAT THE MAGNETIC DISKETTE(S) ON WHICH THE CODE IS RECORDED IS FREE FROM DEFECTS IN MATERIAL AND FAULTY WORKMANSHIP UNDER THE NORMAL USE AND SERVICE FOR A PERIOD OF NINETY (90) DAYS FROM THE DATE THE PRODUCT IS DELIVERED. THE PURCHASER'S SOLE AND EXCLUSIVE REMEDY IN THE EVENT OF A DEFECT IS EXPRESSLY LIMITED TO EITHER REPLACEMENT OF THE DISKETTE(S) OR REFUND OF THE PURCHASE PRICE, AT AP'S SOLE DISCRETION.

IN NO EVENT, WHETHER AS A RESULT OF BREACH OF CONTRACT, WARRANTY OR TORT (INCLUDING NEGLIGENCE), WILL AP OR ANYONE WHO HAS BEEN INVOLVED IN THE CREATION OR PRODUCTION OF THE PRODUCT BE LIABLE TO PURCHASER FOR ANY DAMAGES, INCLUDING ANY LOST PROFITS, LOST SAVINGS OR OTHER INCIDENTAL OR CONSEQUENTIAL DAMAGES ARISING OUT OF THE USE OR INABILITY TO USE THE PRODUCT OR ANY MODIFICATIONS THEREOF, OR DUE TO THE CONTENTS OF THE CODE, EVEN IF AP HAS BEEN ADVISED OF THE POSSIBILITY OF SUCH DAMAGES, OR FOR ANY CLAIM BY ANY OTHER PARTY.

THE RE-EXPORT OF UNITED STATES ORIGIN SOFTWARE IS SUBJECT TO THE UNITED STATES LAWS UNDER THE EXPORT ADMINISTRATION ACT OF 1969 AS AMENDED. ANY FURTHER SALE OF THE PRODUCT SHALL BE IN COMPLIANCE WITH THE UNITED STATES DEPARTMENT OF COMMERCE ADMINISTRATION REGULATIONS. COMPLIANCE WITH SUCH REGULATIONS IS YOUR RESPONSIBILITY AND NOT THE RESPONSIBILITY OF AP.

Chapter 1

Defining the Pointer

In C++, *a pointer is a special variable that holds a memory address.* That's all. Pointers may be treated like standard variables in many ways, but *special* also means that they can behave a bit differently in some operations. Pointers can be used in high-powered constructs for which no other standard variables can be used. There are many familiar aspects to pointers and several that will be unfamiliar to those programmers who are not accustomed to using them. Careless (though technically correct) use of pointers can easily result in a program enigma that is nearly impossible to understand.

It is highly advantageous to review some C++ programming basics, especially in regard to addressing and memory allocation before moving into the topic of pointers. Pointer operations cannot be fully understood until the general storage methods used in C++ are clear to the programmer. These methods and rules are handled by the compiler and are relatively invisible to the programmer. By observing only what *seems* to be taking place, it is quite easy to form misconceptions. Such untruths and half-truths can multiply into total learning chaos through the faulty use of pointers.

Let's begin the discussion by using the following simple program as an example.

```
#include <iostream.h>
int main()
{

    int i;

    i = 34;

    cout << i << endl;

}
```

Here, *i* is declared an auto variable of type int. It is assigned an object value of 34, and its contents are displayed on the screen using the cout stream. Nothing could be simpler. However, to fully comprehend pointer operations and to gain a better understanding of the internal processes that take place within a C++ program, it is necessary to dissect each of the operations carried out under main().

When the int variable is declared, 2 bytes of memory are allocated to store numbers within the standard integer range. (Note: 2-byte integer storage allocation is common for most MS-DOS machines running the most popular C++ compilers. The use of such compilers and systems is assumed throughout this book.)

These 2 bytes are allocated somewhere in memory when the program is executed. The exact location of this memory address is unimportant to the operation of this particular program. The program knows the address of the 2 bytes exclusively allocated to the int variable. It is not necessary that the programmer know this location, only that it exists.

The assignment line in the source code causes the computer to store an object value of 34 in the 2 bytes allocated exclusively for variable *i.* This decimal value is encoded as a 2-byte integer.

Using this coding scheme, the first byte is 34, and the second byte is 0. This is the 2-byte integer coding for a value of 34 decimal. Other combinations allow the 2 bytes to represent values over the range of -32768 to +32767.

When the value in variable *i* is output to the cout stream, the object value of 34 is displayed on the screen as a decimal integer. In C++, decimal values are the default. Hex and oct values require special manipulators.

This is a very simple program, but it is necessary to explore each aspect of its operation, especially in regard to how memory is set aside for storage. This will become more and more important as the subject of pointers is fully entered.

As discussed, the declaration of *i* as a variable of type int causes 2 bytes of private storage space to be set aside exclusively for this variable. The starting address of this small block of memory can be found by using the address-of operator (&) in front of the variable name. The following program demonstrates the use of this operator.

```
#include <iostream.h>
int main()
{

    int i;

    i = 34;

    cout << unsigned(&i) << endl;

}
```

In the cout stream argument, preceding the variable name (*i*) with the ampersand causes the memory location, also called the starting address, of the variable to be returned instead of the value of the integer coded into this memory location. This gets into what are generally termed *lvalue* (left value) and *rvalue* (right value) designations. The first is the memory address of the variable. The second is the object value stored at that address. The &*i* designation is a *pointer* to the address of storage set aside for the variable. &*i* will always point to the address of storage that was automatically allocated to store assignments to variable *i*. This address is fixed and cannot be changed.

Note that the pointer is cast to an unsigned integer in the cout stream. This displays the memory address as an integer instead of a hexadecimal value, the default condition for memory address displays using the cout stream. For tutorial purposes, it is far easier to work with decimal values that state the address location as an offset of the 64K data segment than to use hexadecimal notation.

The unsigned casting is necessary because the offset memory address is probably at the high end of the 64K segment used by most small-memory model C++ compilers, placing it beyond the range of a signed int. The actual address returned by &*i* can vary and depends on machine configurations, operating systems, compilers, and memory usage. Regardless of the value returned, this is the memory location that has been reserved for the exclusive storage of values assigned to variable *i* in the sample program under discussion.

With the model hardware/software used for researching this book, the sample program will return a value of 65524. This means that bytes 65524 and 65525 within the 64K segment of memory were set aside exclusively for storing the integer values assigned to variable *i*. Referring to the first program example where *i* was assigned a value of 34, peeking into memory locations 65524 and 65525 would yield values of 34 and 0, respectively. Remember that an int variable is allocated 2 bytes of storage using most small-memory model compilers designed for MS-DOS systems.

This 2-byte coding (34 and 0) yields a decoded value of 34 decimal. If the value assigned to variable *i* were changed to 1990, then the 2-byte coding would be 198 and 7, respectively; that is, the first byte assigned to variable *i* would be equal to 198 and the second byte would be set at a value of 7. This is the 2-byte coding for a decimal value of 1990.

The key point of this discussion is that *i* is a declared variable of type int and that *&i* is really a constant during any single run of the program. It cannot be changed, because it is directly tied with variable *i* and equates to a value that names the start of the address location set aside for the exclusive storage of assignments to this variable. Its storage allocation is fixed. Thus, the following expression is obviously illegal.

```
&i = 43681;
```

&i can only do one thing. It returns the starting address of the small memory block allocated exclusively to variable *i*. This is a very important fact that will be discussed in greater detail later.

For a clear understanding of pointer operations, it is essential to know that there are two distinct values associated with all variables. (Note: Register variables are an exception and do not hold closely to the direction of this discussion.) The value with which programmers are most familiar is the object value, or the value that is assigned by the programmer, as the following statement demonstrates.

```
i = 34;
```

In this example, the object value is 34, and it is stored at the memory location specifically allocated to variable *i*. The second value associated with all variables is the memory address, the numerical location in memory where storage is allocated for the variable. The designation *&i* should not be viewed as an extension of the variable. It should be considered a constant, which cannot be reassigned. It is fixed. The address-of operator (&), when used with the variable name, causes its address to be returned.

Recalling the definition of a pointer (a special variable that stores a memory address and nothing else), *&i* would seem to qualify. Its memory location value is fixed. The *&i* designation can be used as the argument to a function that is looking for a pointer argument, and it does point to a place in memory. But this is only one expression of a pointer in C++. This is a *fixed* pointer, as it is inextricably linked to the memory location of variable *i*.

Newcomers to C++ who are not familiar with the ANSI C environment are especially cautioned about the dangers of uninitialized (unassigned) variables. In some other languages (such as BASIC), the object values in all numeric variables are initially set to 0 (zero) upon declaration. String values begin life with values of NULL (0) as well.

In C++, the situation is completely different. When an auto variable is declared, only one basic operation takes place. Storage space is allocated exclusively for that variable. The allocated bytes at this memory location are not cleared or reset to zero as in BASIC. Whatever bytes happened to reside at the address where storage is allocated will remain intact.

Knowing this, when the int *i* variable was declared in an earlier program, the contents in the bytes at memory location 65524 and 65525 (2 bytes per int) could have been equal to any value from 0 to 255. If the programmer should mistakenly assume that the starting value in *i* is 0, then numerous problems can occur. The initial value of a declared variable, such as int *i*, has as much chance of being equal to 0 as it does of being equal to any other number within the legal integer range (-32768 to +32767).

This is especially important when dealing with declared pointers, because they can point to any memory location when they are first created. All a pointer can do is return an address in memory. What is done with or at this memory address is up to the programmer.

When an auto variable is declared, it must be remembered that the memory that is automatically allocated for its use may be considered safe storage. Different portions of computer memory are reserved for different purposes when a program is loaded and executed. Some of these areas deal with program management and interface with the operating system. This area is the framework that allows the program to be properly executed. Storage for variables is not allocated in such areas because it would interrupt the framework and result in a program breakdown. Therefore, a large area of memory is allocated exclusively for variable storage. Within this large block, separate allocations for each program variable are made.

However, pointers are not limited to containing addresses within this preallocated block. They may be assigned addresses that lie far outside of this safe area of memory. Writing objects to such unsafe areas by using the pointer as a reference can result in execution catastrophe.

Visualizing Pointers

To learn a complex subject, readers must be able to visualize the intricate processes, preferably in real-world images. One of the best methods of visualizing pointers is to think of houses. Each house has a street address, and each house has one or more rooms. A char house has only one room, since 1 byte of storage is allocated to a char type. A house of type int has two rooms, a float has four, and a double has eight rooms, each room equating to 1 byte of storage.

The single variable, int *i*, is likened to a house that has two rooms, each capable of holding (storing) a single byte of data. In the neighborhood where this house is found are thousands of other homes. The home that represents a long integer is larger than an int home. It contains four separate rooms, each holding a byte of information. The largest home is that of type double that has eight rooms for holding a double-precision floating-point value. In representing character arrays, we might think of a row of townhouses, each containing a single room.

The following program further explains the various neighborhood designations.

```
// ELM Street
#include <iostream.h>
int main()
{

        int i;
        double d;long l;

        i = 57;d = 514.99812;l = 123000;

        cout << unsigned(&i) << endl;
        cout << unsigned(&d) << endl;
        cout << unsigned(&l) << endl;



}
```

The neighborhood for this program consists of three houses. Each is located on the same street, and each has a different number of rooms. Problem! We know that the houses are located on ELM Street, but we don't know what their respective addresses are. The cout stream, as used in this program, can be likened to a neighborhood directory. The *&i*, *&d*, and *&l* designations are the addresses themselves. Therefore, at the beginning of each street in this fictitious neighborhood is the cout directory with a movable arrow, or pointer, with which to point to the names of the houses. When the arrow is aimed at the house designated as *i*, the directory displays the proper address of 65504 ELM Street. When the pointer is aimed at the name of the *d* house, its address of 65506 is displayed on the directory. Going through the same mechanics for the *l* house, we find that it is located at 65514 ELM Street. (Note: These addresses are relatively arbitrary. The important element to this discussion is that whenever the pointer that is a part of the street directory is aimed at a house name, the address of that house is returned.)

The following program is an expansion of the previous example.

```
// ELM Street
#include <iostream.h>
int main()
{

    int i;
    double d;
    long l;

    i = 57;
    d = 514.99812;
    l = 123000;

    cout << unsigned(&i) << endl;
    cout << unsigned(&d) << endl;
    cout << unsigned(&l) << endl;

    cout << sizeof(i) << endl;
    cout << sizeof(d) << endl;
    cout << sizeof(l) << endl;


}
```

The added collection of three cout stream references provides another type of directory. The sizeof() operator allows for the listing of the number of rooms each house contains. This separate directory reveals that the *i* house has two rooms, the *d* house has eight, and the *l* house has four. These values correspond to 2, 8, and 4 bytes of storage space for integer, double-precision floating-point, and long integer values, respectively.

The program that follows borrows from the previous two examples and includes three additional cout calls. These display the object values in each of the variables. This last set of cout calls might be thought of as another type of directory that reveals the contents of each room in each of the fictitious houses.

```
// ELM Street
#include <iostream.h>
int main()
```

```
      {

              int i;
              double d;
              long l;

              i = 57;
              d = 514.99812;
              l = 123000;

              cout << unsigned(&i) << endl;
              cout << unsigned(&d) << endl;
              cout << unsigned(&l) << endl;

              cout << sizeof(i) << endl;
              cout << sizeof(d) << endl;
              cout << sizeof(l) << endl;

              cout << i << endl;
              cout << d << endl;
              cout << l << endl;



      }
```

These three programs have allowed us to determine the address of each of the variable houses, the number of rooms in each, and the combined contents of the rooms.

Summary

This chapter introduced the essential processes that occur when a variable is declared and assigned. Upon variable declaration, an exclusive area of memory, allocated specifically for storage to variables, is set aside. The number of bytes retained depends on the type of variable and can be as large as 8 bytes when dealing with auto variables in a typical MS-DOS system.

Each variable is associated with two distinct values. The most common is the object value, which is assigned to the variable by program statements. The second value is the memory address of the variable. The latter can be obtained by using the address-of operator

(&) in conjunction with the variable name. Any assignments made to the variable are stored in the bytes that begin at this memory address. While it is certainly easy and necessary to change the object value, since it is generally considered to be the true variable value, it is not possible to change the memory address of a declared variable. This is fixed and can be thought of as a constant after the variable has been declared.

Auto variables, the type most often used in C++ (as opposed to register and static variables), can be equal to any legal value when first declared and before any object values are assigned in the program. In other words, an auto variable has a random object value when first declared, because variable declaration simply causes the compiler to set aside storage space. The space reserved for the variable is not cleared to zero, as is the case in some other languages.

The space allocated for the exclusive storage of each declared variable lies in a safe area of memory. This is a product of the compiler's memory management system. This area of memory is not shared by other services that could overwrite the variable's object values or be overwritten by object value assignments to the variable. Likewise, no two variables will be allocated storage at the same address (again, when dealing with the types of variables discussed to this point). These areas of memory, then, are exclusive and safe from intrusion by other standard variables.

A variable can be assigned any legal object value. When dealing with numeric variables that have been discussed in this chapter, legal value refers to object assignments within the normal numeric range for the type of variable declared. Variable i, for instance, can be assigned a value of 14 and then reassigned a new value of 234. This can go on ad infinitum. However, the memory address of that variable is fixed and cannot be reassigned. If storage for this variable is allocated at memory location 65514, then that is the variable's fixed address for the duration of the program. This cannot be changed.

Chapter 2

A Second Step to Learning Pointers

Chapter 1 discussed some of the processes that take place, invisibly and internally, when declaring auto variables under C++. This forms the start of a learning base from which to proceed into the full subject of C++ pointers. This chapter expands upon that base, broadens it, and makes a smooth transition into the subject of declaring pointers and using them to the best programming advantage.

C++ Strings and Char Arrays

C++ strings or, more appropriately, arrays of characters, are quite similar to numbers and numeric variables. Therefore, the creation and use of character arrays in C++ is the next logical step in exploring pointers. The following program provides an example.

```
#include <iostream.h>
int main()
{

    char c;

    c = 65;

    cout << c << endl;

}
```

This program displays the letter "A" on the monitor screen, but as before, stepping through the invisible processes that take place when this simple program is executed lends an important tutorial advantage. The declaration line states that variable c is of type char. Most MS-DOS microcomputers running popular C++ compilers allocate 1 byte of storage for a char data type. A value of 65 represents the upper case A, while B is 66, C is 67, etc. The assignment line uses the ASCII numeric value, but this statement could just as easily have been written in the following manner.

```
c = 'A';
```

In C++ terminology, the 'A' designation means exactly the same thing as 65. Indeed, 'A' is automatically stored by the compiler as decimal 65. The only reason the 'A' is displayed on the screen as a letter instead of a number is that the variable that contains this value is a char type and is not cast to an int before being handed to the cout stream.

As was discussed in Chapter 1, the address of the 1 byte of storage allocated to char c can be returned by adding the following program line.

```
cout << unsigned(&c) << endl;
```

Since only 1 byte of storage is allocated to a char type variable in most C++ compilers intended for MS-DOS machines, the returned address names this single byte's location.

The most common use of the char data type is in the char array, an array of characters that represents a string. A string is often treated as a single unit in many computer languages, and it can be handled in this same manner in C++. However, C++ does not have a true string variable. A string is actually stored as an array of individual units. These units are

characters or chars, and each character in an array consumes 1 byte of storage in most implementations.

The following program demonstrates a very common use of the char array.

```
#include <iostream.h>
#include <string.h>
int main()
{

    char c[10];

    strcpy(c, "COMPUTERS");

    cout << c << endl;

}
```

This program will display COMPUTERS on the monitor screen.

The invisible events are more numerous in this program. First, *c* is declared a char array
allocated 10 consecutive storage bytes. The programmer has direct control over how much
storage space is set aside, whereas with all previous variables, the storage space was automatically set. As with the single char variable, storage is automatically set at 1 byte per char unit,
but here 10 1-byte array elements are specified in the declaration line. Therefore, 10 *SSU*s
(standard storage units) are allocated.

The reason for the selection of an array subscript of 10 is the fact that the string constant, COMPUTERS, is to be copied into the array. While this constant contains only nine
characters, the extra byte of storage is absolutely essential and is not an extra byte at all. The
only element that makes COMPUTERS a true string in C++ and not just a consecutive
trail of single characters is the operation of strcpy(). This function is used to copy the characters that make up this constant into the memory positions set aside exclusively for array *c*. In
C++, a character string is *a single unit of characters terminated by a NULL character*. The
NULL character is ASCII zero. This character is not seen anywhere in the program, but the
compiler automatically adds it to the end of the constant, COMPUTERS. The strcpy()
function copies this NULL character into the tenth array byte. Therefore, the copy of the
constant is written to the 10 consecutive bytes reserved for *c* as shown below.

```
COMPUTERS\0
```

The '\0' is the NULL character and signals the end of the character string. The NULL
makes this combination of characters a true C++ string, a unit that may be treated as a single

entity instead of a grouping of individual characters.

Don't be confused into thinking that strcpy() purposely tacks on an extra '\0' to the end of the quoted string used as its argument when it copies this string into the reserved memory locations. While this could easily be arranged by writing a new version of strcpy(), it is not necessary. This function is designed to terminate upon receiving a NULL byte but only after the NULL is copied to the new memory location allocated to, in this case, array *c*.

Remember that all constants included in a program that is to be compiled must be written somewhere in memory when the compiled program is actually executed. When the constant COMPUTERS is detected in the source code, the compiler causes it to be written somewhere within the executable code that is produced. When this program is executed, the string constant is written to a safe place somewhere in memory, and it is stored as follows.

```
COMPUTERS\0
```

The compiler actually tacks on the NULL character, although it is never seen in the source code. When the strcpy() function is invoked, it is handed the memory address of this constant and copies the contents from the constant's memory location into the bytes reserved for *c*. This includes the NULL character. As a matter of fact, encountering the NULL character is a signal to strcpy() to stop reading further bytes of information.

When strcpy() has completed its run, there are two COMPUTERS strings in memory. One is the original constant that we will assume, for purposes of discussion, is stored in the bytes that begin at memory address 61000. The second string is the copy produced by strcpy() at, again for discussion purposes only, memory address 64115.

In this example, *c*, used without the braces, is a pointer to the string contained in the array. The cout stream begins at the memory address in *c* and starts reading the contents a single character at a time. It writes each byte to the screen as an ASCII character. It will do this until it intercepts the NULL byte (\0).

The reader may ask why *c* is a pointer of type char. The variable was declared a char array and not, specifically, a pointer. This is a valid question, since there are no ampersands and no specifically declared pointers in this program. The answer lies in how C++ handles char arrays. The construct *c[0]*, for instance, is a bona fide variable. It contains or returns the character in the first position of array *c*. However, when *c* is used without a subscript, it then becomes a pointer to the address of the first character in the string.

A char array name, when used without the subscript brackets, is a pointer to the start of the array storage and returns the memory location of the first byte that is also the start of the string. It does not return the contents of that byte. It returns the byte's address in memory!

It can be safely said that *c[0]* is a variable. It can be reassigned any legal object value, as shown below.

```
c[0] = 66;
```

This statement reassigns the first character in our string the letter B. If this line were inserted into our program between strcpy() and the cout stream, then BOMPUTERS would be displayed on the screen. However, *c* used without subscript brackets is a pointer. It does not return the contents of a byte but the memory address of the start of the string.

The address-of operator cannot be incorporated as shown below to return the address of the first byte in *c*.

```
&c
```

The reason for this is that *c* is already a pointer. However, it can be used with a variable.

```
&c[0]
```

This is perfectly legal. Remember, *c[0]* is a variable and *&c[0]* returns the memory address of this variable, the first byte in the array. This also happens to be the same address returned by *c*, the pointer to the start of the array. By the same token, *&c[1]* returns the address of the second byte in the array. It is a pointer to the address of this second byte.

This program can also be written in the following manner.

```
#include <iostream.h>
int main()
{

    char c[10];
    int i;

    c[0] = 'C';
    c[1] = 'O';
    c[2] = 'M';
    c[3] = 'P';
    c[4] = 'U';
    c[5] = 'T';
    c[6] = 'E';
```

```
        c[7] = 'R';
        c[8] = 'S';
        c[9] = '\0'

        i = 0;
        while (c[i] != '\0')
              cout << c[i++];



  }
```

This program does exactly what the previous one did, but it replaces strcpy() with direct assignment lines. The *while* loop provides a very rough picture of how the cout stream handles byte access when displaying a string on the screen. Within the loop clause, termination instructions are given. The loop will cycle as long as *c[i]* is not equal to NULL. Note that *c[9]* is assigned a NULL value, which equates to decimal zero. The cout stream is used to display a single character on the screen during each loop cycle. On each of these passes, variable *i* is incremented by 1. When *i* is finally incremented to a value of 9, *c[i]* is equal to NULL (zero), and the loop is exited.

The analogy this program bears to the first one breaks down upon close examination. In the latter example, no direct pointer operations were used. In the former, the array variable (used without the subscript brackets) was a true pointer.

When viewing the original program, don't be misled into thinking that *c* returns the string. This is totally incorrect. C++ doesn't really have a true string variable but devises a way whereby functions may access a series of characters until a termination point is reached. This stop is signaled by the NULL character. Again, *c* does not equal COMPUTERS but only returns the memory address where the first character in this string is stored. Functions that accept this pointer are programmed to be smart and know to quit what they are doing after reading the NULL character. The following program helps demonstrate this point.

```
        #include <iostream.h>
        #include <string.h>
        int main()
        {

              char c[10];

              strcpy(c, "COMPUTERS");
```

```
        cout << unsigned(c) << endl;
        cout << c << endl;
        cout << (char *) &c[0] << endl;
}
```

When executed, this program will display the following on the monitor test system used for researching this book.

```
65516
COMPUTERS
COMPUTERS
```

The first value is the memory address of the first character in the array and will vary depending upon the type of machine and compiler used. Regardless, the address is that of the first character in the array. The next program line displays COMPUTERS, because the stream has been handed a char pointer argument that causes the memory address to be accessed and the contents at this address to be read consecutively and continuously until the NULL character is encountered. Next, COMPUTERS is displayed again. Why?

Earlier, it was stated that *c* is a pointer that returns the address of the first element in the array. It was also stated that *c[0]* is a variable and *&c[0]* is a pointer to that variable's memory location. Since this is the first variable in the array, its address is the same as the starting address of the array. In the last cout stream call, the address of *c[0]* was cast to a char pointer. Therefore, it was treated like any other char pointer, and the string was read and displayed. Observe that *c*, the pointer, and *&c[0]*, the pointer, point to the same place in memory. They both return the same memory address.

This occurrence is not unusual. The original C language had this feature written in by its designers, and it has been carried over into C++, which is a superset of C. Using the array name without the subscript is simply a shorthand method of stating the same thing with *&c[0]*. This is easier on the programmer, since less keyboard effort is required, but it sometimes tends to confuse beginners. What does the following program display when executed?

```
#include <iostream.h>
#include <string.h>
int main()
{

    char c[10];

    strcpy(c, "COMPUTERS");
```

```
        cout << (char *) &c[3] << endl;
}
```

The answer is PUTERS. Since the argument to the cout stream is the memory address of the fourth character in the array (remember, the count of array elements begins at 0, not 1), the byte read by the stream begins at the letter P. As was stated before, the stream is only given a starting point in memory to begin reading byte contents. The read operation continues until a NULL character is encountered. Since the read began at P and the NULL occurs after the S, only this portion of the original string constant that was copied into the memory location reserved for array *c* is displayed.

In this context, *c* is a pointer and does not equal any object value (at least in the way we think of objects as opposed to addresses). It returns only the address of a memory location where objects have been written. It certainly does not equal COMPUTERS or even the first letter of this string. It is the equivalent of &*c[0]*, which is also a pointer. Both *c* and &*c[0]* point to the same memory location.

The array is in no way equal to the constant, COMPUTERS. Rather, this array contains an exact copy of the bytes that make up this constant. The constant that was an argument to strcpy() lies at one place in memory, and the copy that was made by strcpy() lies at another. This is extremely important in understanding the pointer operations that will be discussed a bit later. The strcpy() function is aptly named, because it *copies* consecutive bytes of data. If a copy exists, then there must be an original. The constant is the original, and the contents of the array are the copy. Both exist simultaneously in computer memory and at different memory addresses. This is not a figurative statement but actual fact.

Array Bounds Checking

One of the touted weaknesses of the C programming language and of C++ is the lack of array bounds checking. This weakness is the cost of frugal use of memory, which is a strong point of both languages. Lack of bounds checking simply means that no safeguards exist to prevent an array from being overwritten. If a char array is declared with a subscript of 10, then only 10 sequential bytes of memory are reserved for storage to this array. However, if a programmer miscalculates and writes more than 10 characters (including the NULL) to this array, then the excess characters are written into the memory locations that immediately follow the block that was allocated for the array. The 10-element boundary of the array is exceeded, and bytes are written into memory locations not set aside exclusively for this array. When this occurs, what happens?

There is no single answer to this question. If there are few declared variables in the program, then there is a good chance that the unreserved portion of memory that was overwritten by the offending string is not being used anyway, and the program may run in a normal fashion. However, if there are many variables, then the exclusive storage allocated to these others may be overwritten by the long string. This will certainly cause an improper execution sequence. In a worst case scenario, those extra string elements may overwrite a management portion of memory or even interact with other variables to do the same thing. The result can be a crash where the computer simply locks up in a continuous loop and must be re-booted. However, there have been cases where hard disk drives have been erased by disastrous overwrites to interrupt addresses.

Overwriting an array is the exact equivalent of writing a program that simply pokes random values into random memory locations. Anything can happen! Obviously, this situation can bring about possible disasters such as the hard disk example. Programmers must be aware at all times of the boundaries associated with arrays and with the total size of any data that may be written to them.

The following program illustrates what can happen in an array overwrite.

```
#include <iostream.h>
#include <string.h>
int main()
{

    char a[9], b[3];
    strcpy(a, "LANGUAGE");
    strcpy(b, "COMPILER");// Overwrite!!!!

    cout << a << endl;
    cout << b << endl;

}
```

The expectation here is the following display.

```
LANGUAGE
COMPILER
```

However, the strcpy() assignment to array *b* is an overwrite! Three array elements were reserved for storage by the following assignment.

```
char b[3];
```

However, COMPILER consists of eight characters and will consume 8 bytes of storage. We must also take into account the NULL character (\0) for a total of 9 bytes. The array bounds are exceeded, but there will be no error message or warning when the program compiles.

The Borland C++ compiler used for testing all applications in this book yielded the following screen display. Other types of compilers may yield different results.

```
ILER
COMPILER
```

The reason for this aberration lies in the way storage is managed. Using Borland C++, array *a* was allocated 9 bytes of storage at memory location 65516 in the 64K segment. Array *b* was then allocated three storage bytes beginning at 65512. Here is what happened. LANGUAGE was written in memory starting at 65516. Nine storage bytes were required to contain this string, so bytes 65516 through 65524 were utilized. Allocated storage for array *b* began at 65512. However, COMPILER requires 9 bytes for storage and this array was allocated only three. Therefore, bytes 65512 through 65520 were filled with this string. The beginning memory address for array *a* began at 65516, so a portion of array *b* (containing COMPILER) overwrote the exclusive storage area for array *a*. The first four characters in LANGUAGE were overwritten by the last four characters in COMPILER, followed by the NULL byte at the end of this string. Therefore, when the *a* array was handed to the cout stream, the characters at this address were read until the NULL was encountered. This resulted in the convoluted display.

Fortunately, this overwrite example was not disastrous. The error was immediately recognizable and could have been corrected easily by allocating more storage space to array *b*. However, if this program had been more complex, an overwrite of this nature could have led to hours of debugging.

This simple example should provide a very worthwhile lesson in array management, a lesson that will carry over (but magnified 100-fold) when dealing with declared pointers.

Houses, Rooms, and Addresses

In the fictitious neighborhood first discussed in Chapter 1, there is a small town with many houses, some containing a single room and others containing many. The house that represents a char variable has a single room for storing 1 byte of data. The following program continues this story.

```
/* CHARACTERS */
#include <iostream.h>
int main()
{

    char c;
```

```
        c = 'A';

        cout << unsigned(&c) << endl;
        cout << c << endl;
    }
```

We know that the house is named *c*, but we don't know its address. To find the correct address, it is necessary to use the cout electronic directory at the corner of CHARACTERS Street. The ampersand pointer, when aimed at the house name, returns the address.

On this same street, there is townhouse complex where all of the units are tied together but are also separate from each other. This domicile will provide a storybook example of the char array that is demonstrated by the following program.

```
        #include <iostream.h>
        #include <string.h>
        int main()
        {

            char c[9];
            strcpy(c, "COMPILER");
            cout << unsigned(c) << endl;
            cout << c << endl;


        }
```

In this townhouse development, there are nine units, each with a single room. The name of this townhouse unit is *c*. Aiming the pointer on the street corner directory at *c* provides the address of the first townhouse in the complex: (arbitrarily) 65516 CHARACTER Street. Since this is a townhouse complex, the value of 65516 is the specific address of the first unit in *c*. This could be stated in another way: The first townhouse is located at *&c[0]*, the second at *&c[1]*, etc. In each single room in each townhouse, there are residents. These are the object values of 'C', 'O', 'M', 'P', 'I', 'L', 'E', and 'R'. However, the last townhouse (*&c[8]*) is vacant or, more accurately, contains the NULL character (\0). The last call to cout in the previous program represents a special feature that is a part of this townhouse directory. It allows the user to see the residents of each unit. When this directory is implemented, the object in each single room is displayed in sequential order. The contents are sampled as long as there are occupied rooms. However, when the ninth townhouse is reached in this poll, it is empty (NULL). This halts the special directory scan.

Summary

Unlike single-element variables, char arrays offer more sampling variations. The address of the start of the array can be found by using the unbracketed array name (a pointer to the start of array storage) as an argument to cout after it has been cast to an unsigned value. The entire contents of this array are displayed by using its name again, still a pointer, as an uncast argument to cout. The address of any single element in the array can be obtained by using the address-of operator in front of the array name followed by its bracketed subscript. Here, it will be necessary to cast to unsigned again. If the user simply wants to return the object stored by a single array element, the subscripted element name without the ampersand is used for the display of a single ASCII character.

For all intents and purposes, each element in a char array may be treated like a standard variable of type int, except that only 1 byte of storage is allocated instead of two. The combined contents of the array may also be accessed as a single unit. This provides great flexibility, uncommon to many other languages, and should not confuse users who are aware of the two-part nature of character arrays. The first part is that of a group of individual values. The second is the string that is all of these values rolled into a single unit.

Chapter 3

Declared Pointers

A pointer is a special variable that returns the address of a memory location. There is nothing especially mysterious about pointers and what they do, but initial concepts often breed their own mysteries, which may be the real problem with programmers and pointers.

The pointers that have been discussed to this point have been fixed in nature. They have been tied to variables that were declared within the program. This chapter deals with variables that are declared from the onset to be pointers. These variables do not store normal objects. Rather, they store addresses of memory locations. Unlike the pointers discussed previously, these can be made to point to any area of memory.

The following program example demonstrates the declaration and use of pointers in C++.

```
#include <iostream.h>
int main()
{

    int i, *p;

    i = 16;
    p = &i;

    cout << i << " " << *p << endl;

}
```

The declaration line within this program names *i* a variable of type int. The same line also declares that *p* is a pointer. The *indirection* operator (*) is the key here. The declaration indicates that the combination of this operator and variable *p* is an int data type, a pointer that is structured to point to an address in memory that contains or can contain a legal int value.

Next, int variable *i* is assigned a value of decimal 16. The statement that follows then assigns pointer *p* the address of the start of storage allocated to *i*. After these assignments have been made, variable *i* contains an object of 16 and *p* points to the first byte of memory allocated to *i*.

Since the address of standard variable *i* is assigned to pointer variable *p*, the following expressions mean the same thing.

```
&i
p
```

This is the result of the assignment line in the sample program.

```
p = &i;
```

When the cout stream is accessed, it is handed two arguments, an int and an int pointer. The indirection operator is used with the pointer name, which means that the object value accessed by the pointer is to be returned. This value is displayed as an int data type, since the pointer was declared to be an int. The screen will display the following values when this program is executed.

```
16      16
```

These two values are more than equal. They are the *same*, having been accessed from the same memory location. Instead of two different but equal values, this is a single value displayed two times on the screen. When the declarations were made, variable *i* was allocated 2 bytes of storage for a standard integer. Pointer *p* was allocated only enough memory to contain a memory address. This is all a pointer can do. In a standard variable, we have learned to expect an object and a memory address. With a pointer, the object *is* a memory address, and like any other object, its value can be changed. Here is a special variable that seems to have the capability of moving through memory. For the time being, we will embrace this conceptualization.

Using the indirection operator, we can retrieve bytes of data from wherever the pointer is made to point or even write new data to that area of memory.

The simple program under discussion usually leads to more questions than it answers, but it does serve as a suitable start. How is the previous program different from the one that follows?

```cpp
#include <iostream.h>
int main()
{

        int i, p;

        i = p = 16;

        cout << i << "" << p << endl;

}
```

This program declares two conventional int variables and causes the two copies of the constant (16) to be stored in memory. One of these 16s is stored at the memory address set aside for exclusive storage to variable *i*. Another copy is made at the memory address set aside for variable *p*. There are no declared pointers in this program.

The important difference is that this program requires storage space for two int values of 16. Therefore, a value of 16 exists twice in memory, each being separate objects assigned to separate variables. In the program example at the beginning of this chapter, only a single value of 16 existed. It was assigned to variable *i*. Pointer *p* was assigned the memory address of variable *i*. When the cout stream was accessed, it displayed the same value of 16 twice, the first having been assigned as the object to *i*, the second being the same object that resided at the memory location contained in pointer *p*.

The on-screen display using either program will be identical, but the source of the values displayed is different. The first program contained a single object of 16 stored at a single memory location. The latter example contained 16 at two memory locations. (Both programs also contain another value of 16. This is the constant that was written directly into the program.) This is an exercise in the difference between two objects that are equal in value and one object that is displayed twice.

We have just seen how a declared pointer may be used to return the object value from the memory location to which it points. The following example shows how the pointer may be utilized to write a value to the same memory location.

```
#include <iostream.h>
int main()
{

    int i, *p;

    i = 16;
    p = &i;
    *p = 168;

    cout << i << endl;

}
```

When this program is compiled and executed, it will display a value of 168 on the screen. Note that variable *i* is assigned a value of 16 in this program, but when it is passed as an argument to the cout stream, it has been changed. Variable *i* now contains an object value of 168. The reason for this lies in the pointer operation.

After the declaration line, assignments are made. Variable *i* is assigned a value of 16, and pointer *p* is assigned the memory address of this variable. This means that *p* points to the exclusive storage area set aside for variable *i*. However, another assignment line uses the indirection operator in connection with the pointer. This combination is the object value at the memory location. *p* accesses the byte contents at the memory address. At this point, these contents are overwritten with a value of 168. This results in the value of 16 being overwritten with the value of 168. Since this is the area of storage exclusively allocated for *i*, the original object value in *i* has changed. This occurs even though no reassignments were made directly to the *i* variable.

Throughout this discussion of declared pointers, the pointer has been assigned the address of a declared int variable by using the address-of operator (&) in conjunction with the variable name. We have already learned that this operator returns the memory address of the storage set aside for the variable. However, if the specific memory location of this variable is already known, the address assignment to the pointer can be made directly and numerically. The following program illustrates this concept. To fully understand, you must assume that the storage address of int variable *i* is 65514. How this came about is not important, but for the sake of discussion, assume that 65514 is the correct address of variable *i* upon declaration.

```
#include <iostream.h>
int main()
{

    int i, *p;

    p = (int *) 65514;
    *p = 122;

    cout << i << endl;

}
```

When this program is executed, the object value in *i* will be displayed on the screen and this value will be 122. This was assigned to the variable indirectly by simply writing it to the memory location allocated to *i* when the program was compiled. This memory location was explicitly assigned to the pointer as well. Again, we assume for the sake of this discussion that 65514 was the location the compiler allocated for storage to *i*. You will observe that when the pointer is assigned a memory address value, a cast operator is used in the form of (int *). This operator casts the numeric value (an unsigned integer constant) into an int pointer type. Some compilers will issue warnings if this cast operator is not used, and many consider it an error not to include it.

Be aware that the following assignment

```
p = (int *) 65514;
```

is exactly equivalent to

```
p = &i;
```

if the memory address of variable *i* is at 65514 in the 64K data segment.

A Practical Use of Pointers

The program examples to this point have been of very little practical value other than as simple tutorials to teach the basics of pointer operations. The following discussion delves into some practical uses of pointers, utilizing them in constructs where no other type of variable will serve nearly as well.

Every beginning C++ programmer has tried at one time or another to do what is illustrated in the following program.

```
#include <iostream.h>
void change(int);
int main()
{

        int x;

        x = 355;

        change(x);

        cout << x << endl;
}
void change(int x)
{
        x = 34;
}
```

The programmer who wrote this code is trying to change the object value in a variable from within a programmer-written function, which can't be done. When this program is executed, it will display the value of 355 on the screen. This value was initially assigned to variable *x*. The operations that take place within the function have no bearing whatsoever on the object value of the variable that was passed to change().

In C++, arguments are passed to functions *by value*. This means that the value in variable *x* in the above example (355) is passed to the change() function. The function variable, also named *x*, is a discrete entity, having absolutely no relationship with the variable of the same name from the calling program.

Since all arguments to functions are passed by value, the only thing a C++ function can do is return a value to the calling program. It cannot change the object value by acting on the passed value of a standard variable. However, pointers allow us to make the in-memory changes attempted by this aborted attempt. Using pointers, the program could be correctly written as follows.

```
#include <iostream.h>
void change(int *);
int main()
{

        int x;

        x = 355;

        change(&x);

        cout << x << endl;

}
void change(int *x)
{

        *x = 34;

}
```

This program will work as originally intended. The value displayed on the screen will be 34. The program is set up as before, but the change() function is passed the *address* of variable *x*, instead of its object value. Within the definition of the change() function, the passed value is declared a pointer of type int by the following line.

```
void change(int *x)
```

The object value in this memory location, *$*x$*, is overwritten by the value of 34. The function has been able to locate the exclusive storage area for variable *x* in the calling program, change it, and then relinquish control to the calling program. Incidentally, the change() function used the name *x* as its pointer variable just as the former, incorrect example did.

This is certainly not mandatory or even desirable. The change() function could just as easily have been written as follows.

```
void change(int *i)
{

        *i = 34;

}
```

A function is a completely separate program from that managed under main(). The variables, pointers or otherwise, within a function are not the same variables that are contained in the calling program, even though they may have the same names. In this last program, the change() function actually creates another pointer of type int that is assigned the same memory address value as that of the pointer value that was passed from the calling program. There are two pointers, one under main() and one under change(), and both point to the same memory location. Altering the object value stored at this single location has the same effect, regardless of which pointer was used to make the change. The pointer in the function was used to change the value at the memory address allocated to *x* in the main program. The variable in the calling program is handed to the cout stream to display the object value.

Note that the memory address of the variable in the calling program is passed as &*x*, using the address-of operator to obtain the pointer value. In the function, the pointer is simply declared in the standard fashion using the indirection operator. The argument is passed to the function as a fixed pointer (fixed to the variable), whereas the pointer variable within the function is declared a pointer from the start.

The best illustration of the use of a pointer to make value changes to an object in the calling program from within a function is the swap() function, first discussed in Kernighan and Ritchie's *The C Programming Language* (1980). An example of this function is illustrated in the following program.

```
#include <iostream.h>
void swap(int *, int *);
int main()
{

        int x, y;

        x = 10;
        y = 127;
```

```
        swap(&x, &y);

        cout << x << "" << y << endl;

}
void swap(int *a, int *b)
{

        int i;

        i = *a;
        *a = *b;
        *b = i;

}
```

Addresses are passed from the calling program to the swap() function. These arguments are declared int pointers within the function, which also declares an internal variable of type int. The latter is a standard auto variable and not a pointer. Variable *i* is used to temporarily store the object value in *a. When used in this context, *a is the object value of the bytes stored at the memory location pointed to by *a*. The indirection operator dictates this type of return. Next, the object at the memory address pointed to by *a* is reassigned the object value that resides in the memory location held by pointer *b*. The indirection operators are used to access the objects at the memory addresses. Finally, the bytes pointed to by *b* are reassigned the value in *i*. The swap is complete and the program will display the following on the monitor, because the object values of *x* and *y* in the calling program have been swapped.

```
12710
```

Since pointers can be directed to any area of memory, one must make certain such an area is safe. In this context, *safe* means not used for other purposes of which the programmer has no knowledge. In the most recent program examples, declared pointers were always given the address of existing variables as shown below.

```
p = &i
```

In this statement, *p* is a declared pointer and *i* is a declared auto variable. Since storage was specifically allocated to *i* upon its declaration, it's safe for the pointer to point to this memory address. As such, the pointer can be used only to retrieve or to write the object value in *i*. The following program demonstrates a very dangerous use of a pointer that inexperienced programmers sometimes attempt.

```
/* Danger!! Don't execute this program */
#include <iostream.h>
int main()
{

    int *i;
    *i = 44;

    cout << *i << endl;

}
```

In this example, a pointer of type int is declared, followed by an assignment to a value of 10. Never forget that a pointer *always* points to a memory location. When a pointer is used to write an object in memory, as is the case here, we must know *where* in memory that assignment is made. The big question in this example is, *To what or where does i point?* The answer is, *Anybody's guess!*

When an auto variable (of type int for this discussion) is declared, memory is set aside for its exclusive storage. The bytes at this storage location are not cleared to zero and may contain any value on a more or less random basis. The same is true of pointers.

However, the object value of a pointer is a memory address. Therefore, when a pointer is declared, the address it contains can be any random value from 0 to 65535 (assuming use of a small-memory model compiler using 2-byte pointers). Here again is the proverbial crap shoot. If you have ever written and executed a program similar to this example, then you were writing things to memory locations not reserved for that purpose. You were poking around in memory at random!

There is a reasonable chance that, if your program was simple and small like this example, the program executed as expected. However, all this really means is that you got lucky. It is also possible that your machine locked up and had to be re-booted or even that another part of your program was trashed.

When objects are written to random memory locations, anything can happen. This sort of programming error is exactly equivalent to the array overwrite discussed in Chapter 2 and must be avoided at all costs. When a pointer is assigned an address value, then it is properly *initialized*. It points to a specified memory location. Writing object values using uninitialized pointers must be avoided.

Other Numeric Pointer Types

The examples of declared pointer operations discussed to this point have all been of type int. This simply means that the declared pointer expects to point to a memory location that contains or will contain an object value within the range of a standard integer. The swap() function allowed the values of two int variables in the calling program to be exchanged. However, this same function would not work if handed the addresses of double-precision floating-point variables.

In C++, a pointer can be any legal data type, intrinsic, derived, or user-defined in the case of classes. The following program shows how the previous swap() function must be altered to exchange the values of two double variables.

```
#include <iostream.h>
void swap(double *, double *);
int main()
{

    double x, y;

    x = 412.791;
    y = 4.67253849;

    swap(&x, &y);
    printf("%lf%lf\n", x, y);

}
void swap(double *a, double *b)
{

    double i;

    i = *a;
    *a = *b;
    *b = i;

}
```

The only change in the swap() function is that the pointer variables have been declared doubles instead of ints. The internally declared variable *i* is also changed to a double-precision floating-point type. Everything else remains the same. The arguments passed to swap()

are the addresses of double variables declared in the calling program.

While it is proper for the programmer to be thinking in terms of memory addresses when dealing with pointers, it is also important to know what kind of object is to be written or returned via the use of pointers. One would no more expect to read from or assign a double value to a memory location set aside for an int value than to assign the object value of a double directly to an int-type variable.

Void Pointers

The void data type is a null value. This type was first introduced with ANSI C, as it was not a part of the original C language. Any function that does not produce a useful (or needed) return is usually declared to be of data type void.

In pre-ANSI C, pointers of type char were the *generic* pointer types because of their 1-byte access alignment. Functions such as malloc() and calloc() in this earlier language typically returned pointers of type char. In ANSI C and C++, the void pointer type has the same address alignment requirements as a char pointer. Therefore, void pointers are most often used in place of the earlier and less expressive char pointer types where applicable.

Prior to the introduction of void, a pointer of type char was usually incorporated to reference some part of memory without having to be concerned with the type of data stored there. For example, the original version of malloc(), the memory allocation function, returned a char pointer. Under ANSI C and C++, malloc() returns a pointer of type void.

The basic concept behind the void pointer is that of a pointer type that can be used to conveniently access any type of object. This avoids much of the typecasting that would be required if the pointer were of another type such as char. The following program makes use of a void pointer.

```
#include <iostream.h>
int main()
{

    void *v;
    char *c;

    c = "Using Void Pointers";
    v = c;

    cout << (char *) v << endl;

}
```

This program will display the following string.

```
Using Void Pointers
```

The address of the string constant is assigned to char *c, then the address in the char pointer is assigned to the void pointer, *v without casting. In the last program statement, the void pointer is handed to the cout stream to display the string value. It is necessary to cast this pointer to a char pointer, or the cout stream will display the address in the pointer instead of the string. The result is exactly the same as if the char pointer had been handed to the stream.

This proves that a void pointer in C++ can be used to point to any data type. It can be assigned the address from any other type of pointer and does not require casting for such assignments to take place.

Summary

This chapter has dealt with the basics of declaring pointers of numeric data types. Declared pointers may be used to point to the location of the same type of auto variable. This is known as initializing a pointer, causing it to point to a known memory location.

Upon declaration, a pointer is uninitialized, as is the case with a declared auto variable. Therefore, an uninitialized pointer has a random object value, the object being a memory address. An uninitialized pointer may point to any area of memory. This makes it a potentially dangerous item that can wreak havoc with a program.

A pointer is declared for the specific purpose of storing the address of a known memory location. Such a location may be specified by the programmer in two different ways. The direct method entails constructs similar to the one that follows.

```
x = (int *) 65117;
```

In this example, 65117 was arbitrarily chosen. It is assumed that the programmer has a specific need to access this location. The indirect method is illustrated by the following statement.

```
x = &y;
```

Here, x is a pointer and y is a declared variable with automatic storage set aside for its objects.

Both of these methods return a numeric address to the pointer. The first is specified as a constant, while the second retrieves an address by using the address-of operator preceding the variable name. We don't necessarily know the specific address using the latter method, but the pointer does and that's what's important.

Pointers are very useful as arguments to functions that must access memory locations within the calling program. All arguments are passed to C++ functions by value. Without pointers, functions could do no more than pass values back to the calling program. With pointers, functions can change values in memory that affect the calling program.

The use of the indirection operator with a pointer name causes the object value at the memory address in the pointer to be returned. The object value may also be changed by making a new assignment via the pointer name and the indirection operator. When used with this operator, the pointer may be treated exactly like an auto variable of the same type.

A pointer stores nothing except a memory address. This is its object value. It does not store a string, an integer, a double, etc. However, it may point to storage locations for such object value types. A pointer points to a place in memory, and through the use of proper operators, the object value at the address to which it points can be retrieved or written.

A declared pointer is not fixed to point to any single memory location. It can be directed to roam throughout all of RAM. The examples of pointers discussed to this point assume the use of a small-memory model compiler. Using MS-DOS, the small-memory models are confined to a 64K segment of memory for data storage. As such, they cannot be made to point to locations outside of this segment. The reason for this is that small-compiler pointers are allocated only 2 bytes to store a memory address. Within 2 bytes, the maximum unsigned value is 65535. Today, even low-level MS-DOS machines are usually equipped with at least 1 megabyte of memory and most contain 2 megabytes or more. The latter configuration offers memory addresses more than thirty times beyond the range of the 64K limitation placed on small-model compilers.

Some discussions later in this book will involve large-model compilers, but the reader should understand that the small models are most desirable, since they are the most efficient. They produce compiled programs with the smallest object code size that usually execute faster than programs compiled with large models. Sometimes it is necessary to forgo these qualities for the all-memory access feature of the large models. As a rule, however, use the small-memory model compilers wherever possible.

Chapter 4

Char Pointers and Arrays

In C++, a pointer may be declared as any legal data type including char. The char pointer is often used to access character strings. For most purposes, char arrays and char pointers may be treated identically, especially in regard to being passed as arguments to functions. The name of a char array (without the use of the subscripting brackets) is a pointer to the start of that array. In C++, arrays of characters may be treated as strings by terminating the series of characters with a NULL (\0). The NULL is what differentiates a character string from a sequential order of individual characters. The NULL is used for purposes of reading the string as a single unit.

The following program demonstrates the declaration of a char pointer and a potential use.

```
#include <iostream.h>
#include <string.h>
int main()
{

    char a[6], *p;

    strcpy(a, "MACRO");

    p = a;

    cout << p << endl;

}
```

This program will display the string MACRO on the monitor screen, because *p* points to the start of the six sequential bytes of memory allocated to array *a*. As with all pointers, the indirection operator is used when declaring a char type. The strcpy() function copies a string constant into the bytes allocated to the array. Next, *p* is assigned the address of the array. When the argument is handed to the cout stream, it is a pointer to a string in memory.

The address-of operator (&) was not used with the array in making the address assignment to pointer *p*, because *a* is the name of the array and is also a pointer when used *without the brackets*. Therefore, *a* returns an address to *p*. The pointer assignment line could also have been written as follows.

```
p = &a[0];
```

This would assign *p* the same value, since this is the address returned by the original assignment line. You won't see an assignment like this in most C++ programs because it is redundant.

The previous program displays the string referenced by *p* when this pointer is used as an argument to the cout stream. We know that *p*, the pointer, has exactly the same significance as *a*, the array name, which is also a pointer because of the lack of brackets. We also know that the following program statement will return the first character in the string to the cout stream, where it will be displayed as a single character.

```
cout << a[0] << endl;
```
"M"

To do the same thing with the pointer, the following program would suffice.

```
#include <iostream.h>
#include <string.h>
int main()
{

    char a[6], *p;

    strcpy(a, "MACRO");

    p = a;

    cout << *p << endl;

}
```

`" M "`

In order to display the char contained at the memory address referenced by *p* (instead of the actual address value), the argument to the cout stream must be an object value. The designation *a[0]* is an object value and so is **p*, which returns the object value at the single memory location pointed to by *p*. A char is displayed on the screen by the stream, because *p* was declared a char pointer. If it had been declared an int pointer, then the stream would have attempted to display the object value as an int.

The declared pointer must always be initialized. In this case, the initialization is accomplished by making it point to the memory location of a declared array. In this program, we can say that the pointer points to a safe area of memory that is composed of six consecutive bytes, since this is the subscript value of the array. However, this example can be made much simpler and will consume less memory by resorting to the following programming mode.

```
#include <iostream.h>
int main()
{

    char *p;

    p = "MACRO";

    cout << p << endl;

}
```

This program does exactly the same thing as the previous examples in this chapter, but it does not require the declaration of a char array. It does not use the strcpy() function, and it is simpler to write. From a memory standpoint, we are dealing with only a single variable, a pointer.

"But, you assigned a pointer an object value and the pointer wasn't initialized!" That may have been the first reaction the reader had to this program because it would seem that we have done just that. After all, *p* wasn't made to point to a char array declared in the program or (apparently) any other memory location. Or was it?

This program is perfectly correct but confusing, since it seems to go against everything that has been previously stated about the use of pointers. Let's answer the question of initializing a pointer by giving it the address of a specific area of memory instead of the random value to which it points when first declared. It was stated previously that C++ does not make any great provisions for strings. The only difference between a series of separate characters and a string is that the string is terminated by the NULL. This is exactly what occurs when a string constant is a part of a C++ program.

This program uses the string constant "MACRO", which is surrounded by quotation marks. This constant must be stored at a memory location when the program is executed, and it is to this location that *p* is made to point by the following assignment line.

```
p = "MACRO";
```

This doesn't assign to *p* the object value, which is "MACRO", but the *address* of the memory location where this constant has been stored. Therefore, *p* does point to a safe area of memory, the area where the constant is stored. Most programmers can grasp the concept of memory being set aside exclusively for declared variables, but memory is also set aside to store constants. Since a pointer may be directed to point to different areas of memory, it is just as easy to make it point to an area used to store a constant as it is to an area of memory allocated for use by a variable.

This program may even be shortened to the following code.

```
#include <iostream.h>
int main()
{

        cout << "MACRO" << endl;

}
```

In this example, "MACRO" is a pointer. In the earlier program, *p* will contain the same address as "MACRO". If you don't fully understand this, the following program may help.

```
#include <iostream.h>
int main()
{

        cout << unsigned("MACRO") << endl;

}
```

This program will display the memory address where the first letter in the string constant is stored. On the model system used for researching this book, the address displayed is at 174 in the 64K data segment. This storage location will change slightly by also declaring a char pointer as is done in the following program.

```
#include <iostream.h>
int main()
{

        char *p;

        p = "MACRO";

        cout << unsigned(p) << endl;

}
```

On the model system, address 170 is displayed. This means that "MACRO" was stored at locations 170, 171, 172, 173, 174, and the NULL character at 175. One might think that this could be confirmed by printing the address of *p* and the address of "MACRO" in the same cout stream. The following program is an example of how one might try to accomplish this goal, but it won't work!

```
#include <iostream.h>
int main()
{
```

```
char *p;

p = "MACRO";

cout << unsigned(p) << "" << unsigned("MACRO") <<
endl;

}
```

This program doesn't perform in the manner many programmers expect. The mistaken concept in this example is that two identical memory addresses will be displayed on the screen. However, the two addresses displayed are different. Why?

The reason is that two different constants are used in this program. The first use of "MACRO" is not equal to the second use of "MACRO". Although both constants are identical in their character makeup, they are two discrete constants, each stored at a different memory address. Pointer *p* has been assigned the address of the first constant. The address of the second constant is stored elsewhere. Therefore, the address in *p* is different from the address of the constant that is passed to the cout stream. The address in *p* is the same as that of the first constant.

The char pointer in C++ is a valuable commodity that will aid the programmer in many endeavors that include more than displaying or accessing string data. Such pointers are often required as arguments to functions that perform mass peek/poke operations as well as other forms of memory management.

Unlike the int pointer, which can be used to read or write a 2-byte quantity, char pointers address areas of memory 1 byte at a time. A char variable is allocated 1 byte, and a char array with a subscript of six allocates six single and consecutive bytes for its exclusive storage.

It was stated earlier in this chapter that char pointers and char arrays may be treated as the same in many C++ applications. The following program example expands on this statement.

```
#include <iostream.h>
#include <string.h>
int main()
{

    char a[6];
    int x;

    strcpy(a, "MACRO");
```

```
            for (x = 0; x <= 4; ++x) cout << a[x] << endl;

    }
```

This program will display a vertical string of characters on the monitor.

```
            M
            A
            C
            R
            O
```

It does this by accessing each character in the array and treating it as a single entity. The bracketed subscript is advanced by the stepping of the loop so that characters in array positions 0/4 are read independently by each loop cycle. Here, the string value is unimportant (as a string, proper). The idea is to access each character on an individual basis.

This same operation can be performed more efficiently by using a char pointer. The pointer equivalent of the previous program follows.

```
        #include <iostream.h>
        int main()
        {

            char *a;
            int x;

            a = "MACRO";

            for (x = 0; x <= 4; ++x)
                cout << *(a + x) << endl;


        }
```

The key to this operation lies in the use of the indirection operator in conjunction with the pointer value added to the loop variable value. If *a* is a pointer that has the address of a string, then *a + 1* is the address of that same string plus 1. For instance, if the address in *a* is 128, then *a + 1* is equal to 129 or memory address 129. If *a* is the address of the start of a string, then *a + 1* is the address one character into the string. It should be stressed that this incrementation takes place in standard storage units (SSUs). Since the storage unit for a char data type is 1 byte, incrementing a char pointer by (numerical) 1 will increment the pointer address by 1 byte (1 SSU for char types). However, if the pointer is an int type using an SSU of 2 bytes, then incrementing this pointer by (numerical) 1 would result in the pointer address being incremented by 2 bytes (1 SSU for int types).

Likewise, if *a returns the first character in a string, then *(a + 1) returns the second character. The parentheses are necessary to establish order of precedence from a purely mathematical standpoint. The expression *(a + 3) is the same as b[3], assuming that b is a char array whose address is contained in pointer a.

The question often arises as to why the second program is more efficient than the first, since they both do the same thing. The answer is found in the lack of memory use in the second program. The first example declares a char array with 6 elements. This means that 6 bytes must be allocated for exclusive storage to this array. Next, a string constant is used that requires five storage bytes. The contents of the constant are copied to the array storage. Once this procedure is complete, there are two separate strings containing "MACRO" residing in program memory, a total of 10 bytes for program string data.

In the second example using the char pointer, we still have the string constant, requiring five bytes of storage. But we do not have to reserve another five bytes of storage for an array to which this constant can be copied. There is no char array. Therefore, the string data storage requirements of this program are half that of the previous program. Of course, the pointer itself requires 2 bytes of storage, but this still represents a savings of 3 bytes.

Big deal! A lousy 3 bytes! So what? Percentages will be more revealing. The latter program was 30 percent more efficient from the standpoint of string data storage. If we were dealing with 1000 strings, a 30 percent savings is nothing at which prudent programmers will turn up their noses. This is sometimes difficult to comprehend when such simple program examples are used for tutorial purposes. Remember that C++ programs may require thousands, hundreds of thousands, and even millions of storage bytes, depending on the scope and complexity of a particular application. Any reasonable degree of memory conservation could be essential.

There is one other area of efficiency in which the latter program excels. There is no strcpy() function. This function is unnecessary because no copy of the constant is made. The pointer is directed to the memory location of the constant. Since the function does not have to be invoked, the storage required for its source code is not a part of the executable program. Additional memory space is spared, and the execution time required by the strcpy() function is saved. The latter program executes faster and consumes considerably less memory. This is a sizable savings, and program efficiency will increase by the complexity of any applications that require similar programming structures.

Using the small-memory model Borland C++ compiler, the first program, using a char array, resulted in an object code size of 12,779 bytes compared with 12,656 bytes for the pointer version. When C++ applications are executed under MS-DOS, there is always a high overhead, this being the operating system interface that allows the program to be supported and executed. The executable (.EXE) files for these two programs measure 23,384 and 23,299 bytes, respectively, with the pointer version being the smaller of the two. The overall percentage of code size reduction is tiny, but one must remember that the sample programs are about as simple as they can be and still execute. As source code builds in size and complexity, the memory savings to be gained by using pointers is much larger. As the C++ program builds in complexity, the MS-DOS overhead tends to remain at approximately the same size. A much greater savings would be had if many, many operations were to be carried out when comparing the pointer version to the char array example.

The following expression does not change the value of the address in *a*.

```
*(a + 3)
```

The address in *a* is used as an initial address. When a value of 3 is added to this base address, an offset of 3 bytes is programmed. However, there is a slightly simpler method of accomplishing the same operation of the last program example and save a bit more storage space. The following program demonstrates this method.

```
#include <iostream.h>
int main()
{

        char *a;

        a = "MACRO";

        while (*a != '\0')
                cout << *a++ << endl;

}
```

This method actually changes the value of the pointer. Within the *while* loop the following exit clause is used.

```
*a != '\0'
```

This causes the loop to continue cycling until the character returned by *a is the NULL that is represented by '\0'. This is the char equivalent of numeric 0. In the cout stream, the following expression is found.

```
*a++
```

This is the standard usage of the incremental operator that may be used in front of the variable name or following it. When the incremental operator precedes the variable name, the variable value (memory address, in this instance) is incremented, and then the object value is returned. When it follows the variable name, the object value is returned, and the address is incremented. The latter operation is what is desired in this program. Each time the stream is accessed within the loop, the current object value or character is returned by *a, and then the memory address in a is incremented by 1 SSU. If we assume that "MACRO" begins at address 158, then the 'M' is located at this address. After the 'M' is returned to the stream, the address contained in the pointer is incremented by 1 SSU. On the next pass of the loop, a is pointing to 159. The 'A' is returned to the stream, and the address is incremented again. This continues until the NULL character is read, signalling the end of the string. The loop starts to cycle again, but the exit clause is satisfied. At this point, *a is equal to '\0', and the loop terminates.

This method of stepping the address value in the pointer eliminates the need for the int variable used in preceding programs and saves storage space. Again, the amount in these examples is negligible, but in larger programs, the potential savings that can be had by this type of programming technique is very large.

There is an even more compact way of performing the same operation of the previous program examples.

```
#include <iostream.h>
int main()
{

    char *a;

    a = "MACRO";

    while (*a)
        cout << *a++ << endl;

}
```

This program does not save any additional storage space when compared to the previous example, but it is quicker to write, as all unnecessary source coding is eliminated. The change occurs in the escape clause within the *while* loop. This notation may seem strange, but this is part of the beauty (and the cause of headaches for beginners) of the C++ syntax.

The escape clause within the *while* loop is merely a conditional test.

```
*a != '\0'
```

This clause returns a value other than 0 as long as the character in *a* is not equal to numeric 0. Again, the character '\0' and the number 0 are one and the same. The *while* statement will continue looping as long as its escape clause does not equate to zero. When *a* does equal 0, the clause also equates to 0, meeting the criterion of the escape condition, and the loop is terminated. In this example, the fact that the clause returns a 0 when *a* returns a 0 is just a coincidence. If the escape clause in *while* had read

```
while (*a != 65)
```

the clause would equate to zero when the 'A' in "MACRO" was returned. ('A' is equal to ASCII 65.) The clause equates to 0 because the conditional test is not met. This condition states that *a* is not equal to 65. The clause returns a TRUE value of other than 0 as long as the condition of the test is met. However, when *a* is indeed equal to 65, the condition is no longer met, and a FALSE value or 0 is returned.

When manipulating string quantities, we are always checking for the end of the string, which is numeric 0. We can use the terminating NULL value to advantage when writing C++ programs that access strings. This is exactly what has been done with the last program example.

We know that the last character in a string is '\0' or numeric 0. Instead of going to the trouble of writing an escape sequence that evaluates the return value of a clause, let's simply evaluate the true value of the pointer object. Therefore, *while* evaluates the content in *a*. As long as this value is not 0, the loop continues to cycle. When the NULL character is read, the numeric value is 0 and the loop is exited. The *while* loop will continue to cycle as long as it reads a value other than 0.

It is important to remember that these last examples have incremented the address stored in the pointer. When the loop is exited, the pointer no longer has the address of the start of the constant. Rather it contains the address of the NULL character at the end of the constant string. This can be proven by the following program.

```
#include <iostream.h>
int main()
{

    char *a;

    a = "MACRO";
    cout << unsigned(a) << endl;

    while (*a)
        cout << *a++ << endl;
```

```
cout << unsigned(a) << endl;

}
```

On the model machine for this book, this program will display the following.

```
170
M
A
C
R
O
175
```

The breakdown on storage of the string constant is shown below.

```
    M    A    C    R    O   \0
   170  171  172  173  174  175
```

The pointer that was initially assigned the address of 170 now contains a value of 175. The latter value is where the NULL character is stored. Programmers must remember that when the address value in a pointer is incremented, its object value, which is the initial address, is changed just as the object value of an int variable is changed when it is incremented.

   This condition makes no difference to this program since it terminates immediately after the loop is exited. Also, when a pointer becomes an argument to a function, the variable that represents this function argument is not the same pointer that was handed to the function. It is another declared pointer that contains the same address of that in the function argument.

   The pointer that is incremented within a function does change its memory address value, but this does not change the address value of the pointer from the calling program. Arguments are passed to functions by *value*. A pointer passes the value of the address it contains. This value is assigned to the pointer declared within the function. Any changes in the initial value passed to the function are in effect only within the function body. Values passed from calling programs are not altered. This applies to pointers as well as to auto variables. However, when a function has a memory address it can write changes into that address. The following program will further explain this concept.

```
#include <iostream.h>
void vert(char *);
int main()
```

```
{

    char *a;

    a = "MACRO";

    cout << a << endl;

    vert
    count(a);

    cout << a << endl;

}
void vert(char *p)
{

    while (*p)
        cout << p++ << endl;

}
```

On the test machine, this program displays the following.

```
170
M
A
C
R
O
170
```

This confirms that "MACRO" is stored at relative memory address 170 and that *a* points to this address before entering the vert() function. The address in *a* is passed to this function as a value that is then assigned to *p*, the char pointer that is declared within the function.

The print operation takes place within the function body by incrementing the address value in *p*. When the function is exited, *p* contains the address value of 175, the NULL character position in the constant's storage area. However, the address value in *a*, the argument pointer, remains unchanged. The major emphasis here is that *a* is not passed to the function. The memory address value in *a* is passed as a value. The memory address is that of "MACRO" and this location is accessed by *p*, which initially points to the same object as *a*.

As programmers learn more about pointers, some misconceptions are bound to creep into the regimen. It is not uncommon to see a program similar to the one that follows.

```
#include <iostream.h>
#include <string.h>
int main()
{

    char *a;

    strcpy(a, "MACRO");

    cout << a << endl;

}
```

This program is totally incorrect and representative of the most common mistake made by C++ programmers making initial excursions into pointer operations.

To what does *a* point? You don't know the answer to that question and neither do I. This is a prime example of overwriting memory. When *char *a* is declared, it points to a random location in memory. In computer jargon, we can say that *a* points to garbage as soon as it is declared. However, one person's garbage may be another person's treasure. The same applies here. One program operations's garbage may be another's exclusive memory area.

Throughout this book it has been stated over and over that when you overwrite computer memory, you're involved in a game of logic Russian Roulette, and the outcome can be almost anything. The program may work or seem to work perfectly. If this occurs, then the hammer fell on an empty chamber. On the other hand, the computer could have locked up or, worse, returned inaccurate information. Bingo! The hammer fell on a loaded chamber. While such occurrences rarely bring about disaster when using small-memory model compilers, large-memory model versions may allow a memory overwrite to trip a few interrupts and, maybe, erase the file allocation table (FAT) on your hard drive. Double Bingo! You've just rendered your entire hard disk useless!

Another common and absolutely incorrect use of a char pointer is demonstrated in the following program.

```
#include <iostream.h>
int main()
{

    char *a;

    cin >> a;

    cout << a << endl;

}
```

Here again is the notorious memory overwrite. The cin stream retrieves characters from the keyboard and stores them in memory. The key word here is *store*, which means that there must be room to put something somewhere. Where in memory are the keyboard characters to be put? The answer is that they will be stored in the series of memory locations beginning at the address pointed to by *a*. But to where does *a* point? To anywhere!

A pointer must always be initialized by assigning it a memory address! This applies in every case. The address can be specified directly as a numeric value or, as is more often the case, it can be named indirectly by assigning the declared pointer the address of a variable or other program entity such as a constant.

Any attempt to *copy* something to a pointer is a mistake. A pointer can be assigned only a memory address.

All of the previous incorrect examples of pointer usage tried to copy bytes of data into unknown memory locations. The proper type of variable to be used in this program for copying char string data is a char array, sized to meet the maximum string input from the keyboard. It is important to know that, once a char pointer is given the address of a char array, the pointer points to a safe area of memory for storage of up to the maximum amount of characters specified in the array subscript. The following program demonstrates this concept.

```
#include <iostream.h>
int main()
{

    char a[40], *p;

    p = a;

    cin >> p;

    cout << p << "" << a << endl;

}
```

This program will accept a keyboard input of up to 39 characters (plus the NULL) safely. The array can store 40 bytes without overwriting memory. The pointer, *p*, is given the address of the array, causing it to point to 40 safe bytes of memory. When this program is executed, a keyboard input of

```
MONITOR <Enter>
```

will result in

```
MONITORMONITOR
```

written to the display screen. This occurs because the pointer serves as the sink for the cin stream. The bytes input at the keyboard are written to the storage area to which *p* points. Since this is the area allocated for *a*, the string is copied into this array. Both *a* and *p* will return the same character string to the cout stream.

Admittedly, this program would be more efficient without the pointer (in this particular example) and would best be written as follows.

```cpp
#include <iostream.h>
int main()
{

        char a[40];

        cin >> a;

        cout << a << "" << a << endl;

}
```

This example writes the same information to the screen, and works in exactly the same manner, since in the previous example both *p* and *a* pointed to the same memory location.

Can you deduce what the following program will display on the monitor?

```cpp
#include <iostream.h>
#include <string.h>
int main()
{

        char a[40], *p;

        strcpy(a, "MICROPROCESSOR");

        p = a;

        strcpy(a, "DISKETTE");

        cout << p << endl;

}
```

If you answered MICROPROCESSOR, then you are wrong. The right answer is DIS-KETTE. Pointer *p* is given the address of the start of array storage. It is not made to point to either of the two string constants, only to the start of array storage. When *p* is assigned the address of *a*, it immediately points to the first string copied into *a*. The bytes that make up MICROPROCESSOR were stored in *a* at the time of this initial assignment. However, the next program operation copies a new string into *a*. DISKETTE overwrites MICROPRO-CESSOR. The pointer still points to the memory address of *a*. Therefore, *p* now points to DISKETTE, which resides at the same location previously used to store MICROPRO-CESSOR.

When a pointer points to the address of an array, it is totally interchangeable with the array as far as arguments to functions such as strcpy(), strlen(), etc. are concerned. Some would say that *p* is equal to anything *a* is equal to. This is correct but can also be misleading. Since both *p* and *a* are pointers (remember, the array name becomes a pointer when used without the subscripting brackets), they contain the same memory address. However, it is more accurate to say that when a declared pointer is given the address of an array, the contents of the array and the object that the pointer accesses are always the same.

There is a big difference in a variable being equal to a value and in one being the *same* as that value. The following program demonstrates this difference.

```
#include <iostream.h>
int main()
{

    char a[40], *p;

    strcpy(a, "GARAGE");

    p = "HOUSE";

}
```

The string constant, "GARAGE", is copied into the char array. This causes the bytes that make up the constant to be copied or reproduced in the array. When this copy operation is complete, there are two strings in memory. The first is the constant, "GARAGE", and the second is the copy of the constant, also "GARAGE". Therefore, the contents of the array are equal to "GARAGE", but they are not the same as the constant, "GARAGE". The constant resides at one memory location, the contents of the array at another.

In contrast, the pointer is assigned the memory address of the constant, "HOUSE". No copy takes place. "HOUSE" is found at only one location in program memory. Therefore, *p* points to "HOUSE", the constant. In this regard, they are one and the same. The address of "HOUSE" and the address to which *p* points are identical.

In human terms, we can compare this example with identical twins. They look alike. You can't tell the difference in the two when they stand side-by-side. However, there are two of them. They are not one and the same. In the above example, "GARAGE" was twinned. By the same token, "HOUSE" is an individual. Only one exists. Therefore, anything that equates to "HOUSE" is "HOUSE" and not a copy.

Arrays of Pointers

At this juncture, we have compared char arrays to char pointers. An array is a collection of single data units, while a pointer is a special variable that stores the address of a memory location. However, arrays of pointers are not only possible but also practical. The following program establishes a base for these discussions.

```
#include <iostream.h>
#include <string.h>
int main()
{

    char a[5][15];
    int x;

    strcpy(a[0], "DATA");
    strcpy(a[1], "LOGIC");
    strcpy(a[2], "MICROPROCESSOR");
    strcpy(a[3], "COMPUTER");
    strcpy(a[4], "DISKETTE");

    for (x = 0; x <= 4; ++x)
        cout << a[x] << endl;

}
```

This program simply copies five string constants to the two-dimensional array, *a*. In making the declaration, the second portion of the subscript determines maximum string length. Since we know that "MICROPROCESSOR" will be the longest string and that it contains 14 characters, the minimum string length declared for the array is 15 characters or bytes. This will be just large enough to contain the 14 characters in "MICROPROCESSOR" plus one more byte for the NULL character.

The multidimensional array can also be classified as an array of strings or even as an array of char arrays. However, the array declaration does not allow for dimensioning to address different string lengths. If the maximum string length is 15 bytes, then storage of this quantity is provided in all five of the subscripts. This applies even though most of the strings are fewer than eight characters long. Providing 15 bytes for each string is a waste of storage. The strcpy() function is used to make a copy of the string constants and to store them in the bytes allocated for each string in the array.

A *for* loop is entered, which causes the contents of the array to be written to the screen. This is a multidimensional array, so the expression *a[x]* is a pointer to the *x* element or *x* string in the array. This may seem to conflict with earlier discussions that stated that the array variable name without the subscript brackets was a pointer, while the array name with brackets returned the object. This applies only to single-dimension arrays. With two dimensions, a single set of brackets with the name is a pointer, while the following construct returns the object at the array position specified by the values of *x* and *y*.

```
a[x][y]
```

The expression

```
a[0]
```

where *a* is a multidimensional array, is a pointer to the first element of the first string in the array. *a[1]* is a pointer to the first element of the second string, etc.

In addition to the wasted memory usurped by the array that must size all elements to the length of the largest is the storage required for constants as well as for copies of those constants. This is a most unsatisfactory condition and should be remedied through the use of string pointers. This approach is demonstrated in the following program.

```
#include <iostream.h>
int main()
{

    char *p[5];
    int x;

    p[0] = "DATA";
    p[1] = "LOGIC";
    p[2] = "MICROPROCESSOR";p[3] = "COMPUTER";
    p[4] = "DISKETTE";

    for (x = 0; x <= 4; ++x)
        cout << p[x] << endl;

}
```

This program declares an array of char pointers. The following designation declares *p* an array of five char pointers.

```
char *p[5];
```

The pointer to the first string is *p[0]*, the second string *p[1]*, the third *p[2]*, etc. Nothing is copied to the pointers in the array. Only memory addresses are assigned. Each of the five pointers in the array is assigned the address of a constant, avoiding the copy procedure from the previous program and eliminating the doubled storage requirements. The remainder of the program proceeds in a fashion that is identical to the previous example. The execution run will be identical to the one that used the multidimensional char array.

However, from a memory usage standpoint, this program is very different. Using the Borland C++ compiler on the test computer, the multidimensional char array version consumed 13,239 bytes in object code format and 24,305 bytes as an executable file. The pointer version of this same program required only 13,089 bytes for the object code and 24,192 bytes for the executable file. This is still not highly significant, but storage savings definitely grow as program complexity increases.

Summary

C++ char pointers are the most common of all. Char pointers are closely aligned with char arrays, and the two can be used interchangeably in many applications. However, there are very significant differences in the two regarding storage techniques and memory consumption. Char arrays are allocated storage based upon the subscript values specified by the programmer and are used to *store* data.

Char pointers are allocated no storage areas for common objects (in this case, char data). The only object a char pointer can store is a memory address. Upon declaration, a char pointer automatically contains the address of a random memory location. This uninitialized address value should be considered garbage, useless for any practical programming purpose.

Only when the char pointer is assigned an address does it become initialized. It then points to a place in memory specified directly or indirectly by the programmer. Any variable, pointer types included, is useless and dangerous when it contains a random value. It is always necessary to give the pointer something at which to point. False assumptions about the address contained in a pointer can lead to, at minimum, a faulty program that is very difficult to debug. In a worst case scenario, data may be written to a protected memory location, creating havoc with the operating system interfaces.

A char pointer expects to point to a memory location allocated to data of type char. This equates to one byte of storage for one character in most MS-DOS systems. Char pointers are often used as an efficient means of manipulating string constants. They may also access the storage areas of char arrays. In the latter usage, they may be treated just like arrays. The important concept here is that the char pointer must always contain the memory address of a safe area of memory, one designed for char or char string operations.

Chapter 5

Memory Access via Pointers

Since pointers have the ability to point to different areas of memory and to read and write information at these locations, they would seem to be the ideal instruments for performing manipulations in and to memory. Every computer language contains some mechanism that will allow a memory location to be accessed for the purposes of returning the byte content from that location or to alter the byte in that location. Such mechanisms are usually called peek/poke devices.

All of the discussions to this point have used program examples that were compiled using the small-memory model version of the Borland C++ compiler. Small-model compilers restrict memory access to a 64K data segment unless special *far* pointers or functions are used. This chapter explores large-memory model compilers and *far* pointers. However, the beginning discussions still use the small-memory model, which is adequate for introduction purposes.

The following program is a partial repeat of several others from Chapter 4 but is examined in a different light.

```
#include <iostream.h>
int main()
{

        char *a;

        a = "CAT";

        cout << int(*a) << endl;

}
```

The argument to the cout stream is cast to an int type. This displays the object value in *a as a decimal integer. The value displayed on the screen will be 67, the ASCII code for 'C'.

We know that pointer *a* is given the address of the constant in the following assignment line.

```
a = "CAT";
```

Assume for the purposes of this discussion that the storage location for the constant begins at address 170 in the 64K segment. What has this program done? It has *peeked* into memory location 170 in the segment. The byte value at this address is 67. This clearly demonstrates that all a peek consists of is returning the byte value from a specified memory location.

The original C language contained a peek() function, and this has been carried over into ANSI C and C++. Most C++ compilers also offer specialized functions that will peek into memory and return data in various formats. The latter are not portable functions, as they are specially tailored to a particular brand of compiler. However, a peek function in C++ is redundant, since pointers allow easy access to memory through direct programming methods that are far more efficient than using functions to accomplish the same task.

The following program demonstrates a *poke* operation.

```
#include <iostream.h>
int main()
{

        char *a;

        a = "CAT";

        *a = 66;
```

```
        cout << a << endl;

}
```

When this program is executed, it will display

```
BAT
```

The following assignment line within the program causes the first byte referenced by *a* to be replaced (overwritten) by the assignment to **a*.

```
*a = 66;
```

The indirection operator causes the specific byte to be returned or, in this case, written by assignment. This is a typical *poke* operation. Pointer *a* points to the memory address where the constant is written, specifically to the first byte in the string at location 170. The expression **a* returns this byte or can be used to write another byte on top of it. In this case, the new byte has a value of 66 and is poked into memory over the initial value of 67. ASCII 67 is the letter 'C' and ASCII 66 is the letter 'B'. Memory has been altered by this poke operation. The cout stream displays the result of the change made in memory as BAT instead of CAT.

Memory Models

Most C++ compilers for MS-DOS machines offer several categories of memory models. These can be classified into two basic categories, small- and large-memory models. A specific compiler may have four or more memory model options that are often classified as tiny, small, and compact, each of which falls into the base category of small-memory models. Large-memory models compilers may have subcategories of medium, large, and huge. For this discussion, the main difference between these two memory model classes is in the default size of the pointers. The small model, which has been used for all programming examples to this point, defaults to 2-byte pointers. Large-memory models default to 4-byte types.

From an execution efficiency standpoint, the small-memory model offers the fastest execution and smallest code size. However, this model also limits its default pointers to 2-byte entities. Such a pointer contains the same storage capacity as an unsigned int. (Note: Byte size for various types of data may vary on different types of computers. Most MS-DOS C++ implementations utilize the same storage parameters as does the model compiler used in researching this book, i.e., 1 byte for chars and voids, 2 bytes for ints and unsigned ints, 4 bytes for floats and long integers, and 8 bytes for double-precision floating-point values.)

An unsigned integer can store a maximum value of 65535 (64K). Any pointer that is declared in the normal manner using a small-memory model compiler is allocated 2 bytes for address storage. This applies regardless of the type of pointer that is declared. Since only two bytes of storage are allocated, the maximum memory address value is limited to 65535. This severely limits the memory that can be addressed, as a typical system may have addresses spreading out to twenty times this amount and more.

The earliest C compilers for MS-DOS machines were available only in small-memory models. Most made no provisions for memory excursions outside of the 64K data segment. Later versions offered special functions that would address any valid memory address. Newer compilers were offered in large- and small-memory models, and still later versions allowed for special 4-byte pointers to be specifically declared from within small-memory models. While C++ is a superset of ANSI C, it has inherited more than the ANSI C language. It is also the benefactor of the evolution that occurred in C compilers and their memory access capabilities. Today, all popular C++ compilers offer small- and large-memory models to address specifically any programming need.

A programmer who wants the fastest possible execution speed will attempt to stay within the confines of the small-memory compiler versions. Prior to software houses including the option of declaring 4-byte pointers in small-memory model compilers, the need to roam around in all of a computer's memory forced the use of the large-memory models with their slower execution speeds and larger code sizes. However, today's C++ compilers offer the option of using a small-memory model while specifically declaring 4-byte or *far* pointers when memory excursions outside of the 64K data segment are desired.

For specific peek/poke operations, C++ compilers also offer special functions. Borland C++ compilers use functions named peekb() and pokeb(). The first returns a single byte from memory based upon segment and offset arguments. The second writes a single byte to memory based upon the same arguments, plus the byte value to be written. Other brands of compilers offer similar functions, although they may be given different names. Such functions are really nonstandard and included in compilers for the convenience of users as opposed to maintaining portability across systems.

Poke Operations

The Borland C++ compiler used as the model for this book offers the pokeb() function to write a single byte to a memory offset with a 64K segment using the small-memory model compiler version. The following program uses this function to cause the 'A' character to appear in the upper left corner of the VGA screen.

```
#include <dos.h>
int main()
{

        pokeb(0xb800, 0, 65);

}
```

The letter 'A' is equal to ASCII 65, which is the value used with the pokeb() function. Since this program is compiled using a small-memory model, only one 64K area of memory can be accessed at a time. This function statement can access any of 65,535 bytes in this segment. We can move through all of memory with this combination. If it is necessary to move outside of the specified 64K segment, the segment value must be changed. In the above example, the first argument value is 0xb800, the address of the VGA screen buffer specified in hexadecimal format. This value is the same as 47104 decimal. The second argument is the offset into the segment. The 0 value targets the first byte at 0xb800. The third argument is the byte that is to be written at the specified memory location.

The pokeb() function serves a purpose, but it is wasteful to use a function to perform this simple operation, especially since we already know that pointers can address any area of memory. The following program must be compiled using the large-memory model of the Borland C++ compiler.

```
// Compile with large-memory model
int main()
{

        char *a;

        a = (char *) 0xb8000000;

        *a = 65;

}
```

Like the previous program, this code also causes the letter 'A' to be written in the upper left corner of the screen. No function has to be invoked, so the program performs its job faster. The poke operation is handled directly by the char pointer. The only unusual feature of this program to some readers will be the address value. One must remember that far pointers, the type created when any pointer is declared in the normal fashion using a large-memory model compiler, are 4-byte entities. With 8 bits to a byte, 2-byte pointers require 16-bit numbers, while 4-byte pointers must have 32-bit addresses. The assignment to the pointer in this program is a 32-bit address, specifically naming the VGA screen buffer segment of memory. In 8-bit terminology, the 32-bit address can be broken down into a segment and an offset.

```
                    SEG   OFFSET
          0x    b800  0000
```

If you are accustomed to providing addresses in 8-bit values, and most users of MS-DOS machines and software are, then follow the hex value with four zeros. Purists will opt for the mathematical method where the 8-bit address is multiplied by 0x10000. If you prefer to work within the decimal system (cumbersome when dealing with memory addresses), then multiply the decimal memory address by 65535.

The previous program must use absolute addressing when dealing with memory locations, and each address is given as a 32-bit (4-byte) quantity. 0xb8000000 is the address of the start of the VGA display buffer. (Systems with the monochrome monitor will use 0xb0000000 to access this screen buffer.) The assignment line uses a cast operator to coerce the numeric value to type char *. This is necessary in type casting the numeric value to a form that is acceptable to the compiler.

Once the assignment of a memory address has been made, *a* points to the start of the screen buffer. This means that *a* will access the object value stored in the byte at this location. The following construct reassigns a value of 65 to this byte.

```
          *a = 65;
```

The letter 'A', which is represented by decimal 65, appears in the upper left corner of the screen. This is far more efficient, both from a programming and an execution speed standpoint when compared to calling the pokeb() function. Calling a function from a program requires additional execution time.

When a C++ application uses a function, the calling program actually relinquishes control to the function. This takes more time than when the code is accessed within the calling program. You can literally see the difference calling a function like pokeb() makes in execution speed when a slow XT-class computer is used. However, modern computers with their high clock speeds won't allow the user to see the speed differential. The following program fills the VGA screen with 'A' characters using pokeb(). The screen is completely filled 1000 times, which provides a sizable enough task to gain some measurable time interval. The Borland C++ gettime() function is used to register the clock time at the beginning of execution and, again, at the end. This information is displayed on the screen in seconds.

```
// Use large model compiler
#include <iostream.h>
#include <time.h>
#include <dos.h>
int main()
{

        struct time tm;
        int x, begin, bsec, bhund, esec, ehund, ct;

        gettime(&tm);
        bhund = tm.ti_hund;
        bsec = tm.ti_sec;

        for (ct = 0; ct < 1000; ++ct)
            for (x = 0; x <= 3999; x += 2)
                pokeb(0xb800, x, 65);
        gettime(&tm);
        ehund = tm.ti_hund;
        esec = tm.ti_sec;

        cout << "Begin-- " << bsec << "." << bhund <<
endl;

        cout << "End-- " << esec << "." << ehund <<
endl;

}
```

This program should be compiled using the large-memory model option to obtain a fair comparison.

The monochrome and color text screens on MS-DOS computers are comprised of 4000 single bytes. Each even byte (including 0) will display a character on the screen when poked with an ASCII value. In this case it is 65 for the letter 'A'. However, each odd byte (1 to 3999) controls screen attributes. The standard screen fills each attribute byte with a value of 7, as this will bring about normal display of each character. Other attribute values will cause the preceding character to be displayed in flashing, bold, or underlined format. Since the screen attribute bytes already contain a value of 7 for normal display, it is unnecessary to address the odd bytes at all in this program example.

The first *for* loop cycles 1000 times. On each pass, the internal *for* loop fills the entire screen with 'A' characters. This latter loop steps variable x from a value of 0 to 3999 in increments of 2. On the first pass of the loop, x is equal to 0. On the next pass, it will be equal to 2, then to 4, then to 6, etc. This allows only the even bytes to be accessed. These are the bytes to which character 'A' code will be written.

The pokeb() function is called on each pass of the nested loop. The segment value is always 0xb800, the 8-bit code for the start of the screen buffer. (Note: If you are using a monochrome monitor, this value should be changed to 0xb000.) The pokeb() function requires an 8-bit address, even when it is compiled by the large-memory model compiler. The stepping value in x is used as the offset argument, and 65 is the byte that is poked into all accessed locations.

On the first pass of the loop, 65 will be poked into byte 0xb000 + 0. On the next pass, the byte location is 0xb000 + 2, then 0xb000 + 4, etc. When the loop times out, all of the character bytes in the screen buffer will be filled with the 'A' character. At this point in the execution chain, the nested loop times out, and the outside loop cycles again. The screen is rewritten using the same process. This occurs 1000 times. Multiplied by the nested loop's 2000 cycles, this equals a total of two million looping operations in the entire sequence. The 33 megahertz 80486 computer used for researching this book required 2.86 seconds to complete the execution of this program.

The next program performs the same on-screen operations, but it does not call the pokeb() function. Instead, it uses direct pointer access to write the screen.

```
// Use large model compiler
        #include <iostream.h>
        #include <time.h>
        #include <dos.h>
        int main()
        {

            struct time tm;
            int x, begin, bsec, bhund, esec, ehund, ct;
            char *a;

            a = (char *) 0xb8000000;

            time(&tm);
            bhund = tm.ti_hund;
            bsec = tm.ti_sec;

            for (ct = 0; ct < 1000; ++ct)
                for (x = 0; x <= 3999; x += 2)
                    *(a+x) = 65;
```

```
                    gettime(&tm);
                    ehund = tm.ti_hund;
                    esec = tm.ti_sec;

                    cout << "Begin-- " << bsec << ":" << bhund <<
            endl;
            cout << "End-- " << esec << ":" << ehund << endl;

            }
```

Compile this program using the large-memory model option as before. On execution, the monitor will again be filled with a full screen of characters. This method of poking in characters is much faster because no function was called. For all intents and purposes, the pokeb() function uses the same principles that this program incorporates. With functions, however, there is a far greater overhead since they must declare additional variables that this program avoided.

If you are using a fast computer, you won't be able to see the speed difference in the two methods, but this difference is quite significant as is indicated by the elapsed time routine. On the model computer, this program completed its execution run in 0.88 second, making it 3.25 times faster than the application that called pokeb(). Even though we are still dealing with fractions of a second, the percentages tell the whole story. The second program exhibited an execution speed improvement of 325 percent over the first!

Newcomers to C++ often become confused over the avant garde use of characters such as 'C', 'f', 'L', etc., interchanging them with numbers. C++ makes no distinction whatsoever between 'A' and the numeric value 65. They are both one and the same. Certainly, functions are available that will display 65 as 'A' or vice versa. The following simple integer assignment may be written in different ways.

```
            x = 66;
```

This is a simple assignment, but the statement below means exactly the same thing.

```
            x = 'B';
```

In both cases, variable x is assigned a value of 66 decimal. How this value is displayed on the screen depends upon casting or the use of various manipulators when using the cout stream. A cast to type char will cause a numeric value argument of 66 to be displayed as the letter B. If cast to type int, then the same value will be displayed as decimal 66. If you go in for hexadecimal numbers, then a stream manipulator of *hex* will cause decimal 66 to be displayed as HEX 42. Similarly, an *oct* manipulator will display this value as octal 102. All of these values — 66D, 'B', 42H, 102-OCT — are equal. The numerical base in which they are displayed is up to the programmer.

Peek Operations

Now that the mysteries of poking bytes into memory have been explained, let's concentrate on peek operations. The process is quite similar, as memory locations are accessed as before. However, instead of writing a byte of data to the address, the byte already in that location is read. The following program demonstrates this operation using the Borland C++ peekb() function.

```
#include <iostream.h>
#include <dos.h>
int main()
{

        int x;

        x = peekb(0xb800, 0);

        cout << x<< endl;

}
```

The function allows the segment to be input as an 8-bit quantity, while its second argument is the offset (number of bytes) into that segment. This function returns a value of type int. The return is the object value of the byte at the location specified. The segment address is the start of the VGA display buffer, so if the letter 'A' appears in the upper left corner of the screen prior to running this program, *x* will be equal to 65, the decimal equivalent of character 'A'.

The following program shows a more efficient method of accomplishing the same thing by directly programming a pointer to handle the access.

```
// Compile with large-memory model
#include <iostream.h>
int main()
{

        char *a;
```

```
a = (char *) 0xb8000000;

printf("%d\n", *a);

}
```

This code must be compiled using the large-memory model option of the C++ compiler. As with the equivalent example of a poke operation, this program declares *a* to be a pointer of type char. This pointer is then given the address of the screen buffer in 32-bit format. However, instead of assigning an object value to *a*, we simply print the value already in *a*. The returned byte is displayed as an integer value, although it could also be displayed as a character, a hex value, or even an octal value if desired. What is contained in *a* is a single value. How it is displayed is up to the programmer.

How would you go about writing your own function to handle a peek operation? The direct method is most efficient, but if you had to write such a function for some unknown purpose, you would simply follow the program logic presented above and end up with something similar to the following source code.

```
int peeker(long loc)
{
        char *mem;
        mem = (char *) loc;
        return(*mem);
}
```

The construction of this code assumes that the address handed to the function (represented here by *loc*) would be a 32-bit quantity and that this function would only be used in programs compiled using large-memory models. A long int type is handed to this function, since this variable can store most memory addresses. A char pointer is declared within the function and is assigned the value in *loc* as an address. Once the pointer is aimed at the right location, all that is necessary is to return the byte.

A small-memory model version of this same function is certainly possible. However, it is first necessary to further examine the features offered by modern C++ compilers.

Far Pointers

One advantage of the small-memory models of modern C++ compilers is the default 2-byte pointers. These offer optimum execution speed and allow for smaller code size. The disadvantage of this model is that the same 2-byte pointers cannot be used to address all memory locations. The programmer must use functions that will address memory, and this results in slower execution speeds.

The advantage of the large-memory model options of the same compilers is that the 4-byte pointers provide full access to all memory addresses. However, using large models will result in slower equivalent execution times and larger code size. A solution to this problem is to use a small-memory model compiler that offers the option of declaring 4-byte pointers.

This is exactly what the best C++ compilers offer. The small-memory models may be used to provide compact code along with the fastest execution speed. All pointers declared in the normal fashion will be 2-byte types. However, if you need a special pointer to access a memory location outside of the code area restricted by the 2-byte entities, then declare a pointer to be a 4-byte type.

Such pointers are declared by using the *far* keyword. The following program is compiled using a small-memory model compiler and illustrates the difference between *near* and *far* pointers.

```
#include <iostream.h>
int main()
{

    char *a;
    char far *b;

    cout << sizeof(a) << endl;
    cout << sizeof(b)) << endl;

}
```

The first pointer, *a*, is declared using standard conventions and, by default, is allotted 2 bytes for storage. The second is modified by the *far* keyword and is a 4-byte entity. All of this assumes that the program is to be compiled using a small-memory model option. The cout stream is used to display the size of each pointer in bytes using the intrinsic C++ sizeof() operator. When the program is executed, you will discover that pointer *a* has a size of 2 bytes and *b* has 4 bytes.

With the option of the *far* keyword, we have the best of both worlds: small-memory model speed and economy, and the ability to declare far pointers to address any area of memory. While the declarations of these two types of pointers were made on separate program lines, this was done only for the sake of clarity. The more obvious method of making these two declarations would be to use a single line.

```
char *a, far *b;
```

This declares *a* to be a standard (2-byte) pointer, while *b* is a far pointer, both of type char. Incidentally, the designation of *far* is quite appropriate and is based upon assembly language nomenclature of *near* and *far* operations. The far pointer is able to gain access far away from the data segment and into other memory areas. The standard 2-byte pointer is called a near type, since it must stay nearby, within a predetermined memory segment.

The following program is the equivalent of the peek operation discussed earlier, but it is compiled under the small-memory model option of Borland C++.

```
#include <iostream.h>
int main()
{

    char far *a;
    a = (char far *) 0xb8000000;

    cout << *a << endl;

}
```

Notice that the cast contains the *far* modifier. Variable *a* is not a char pointer but a *char far* pointer. The address assigned to *a* is expressed as a 32-bit quantity as is required for 4-byte pointers. Other than the addition of *far*, the program is identical to the earlier example and returns the first byte in the screen buffer.

Returning to the previous task of writing a peek function that can be compiled with a small-memory model compiler and that will accept 8-bit addresses, the job is made simple by using the far pointer option. The code for this function is shown below.

```
int peeker(int seg, int off)
{

    char far *mem;

    mem = (char far *) (seg * 65536);

    return(*(mem + off));

}
```

The peeker() function accepts two arguments. Both are of type int. The first is the 8-bit segment address, and the second names the offset into memory.

The following designation simply adds the offset value to the segment value and returns the byte at that address.

```
* (mem + off)
```

This corresponds to the operation of peekb() that was discussed earlier. Another method of writing this same function is demonstrated in the following code.

```
int peeker(int seg, int off)
{

    char far *mem;

    mem = (char far *) (seg << 16) + off;

    return(*mem);

}
```

The altered line in this function is shown below.

```
mem = (char far *) (seg << 16) + off;
```

This is quite a mouthful, but it's easily explained when taken in small segments.

```
seg << 16
```

This portion uses the C++ *left-shift* operator that incorporates the same symbol as the stream operator. The expression means exactly the same thing as

```
seg * 65535
```

However, the former method requires less keyboard input and is more expressive when dealing with HEX values. After this operation takes place, the offset value is added. Therefore, *mem* points to the proper address of *seg*, converted to a 32-bit address, plus *off*. This method is shown because C++ programmers often use short cuts that are not as clear as some of the simpler examples found in this book.

Writing the peeker() function has been an excellent practicum, but we can accomplish the same thing without resorting to a function. The direct method of peeking memory will result in the most efficient programs.

At this juncture in my seminars and C++ workshops, someone invariably asks why char pointers are used for these purposes and not int or long types. That's a good question, and there is a good answer. A char pointer expects a return value of type char or can be used to write a value of type char. (Remember, a char can be specified as the character itself, as in 'A' or as its ASCII code, 67.)A char value is a 1-byte entity. Conversely, int pointers expect an int return that is a 2-byte value on MS-DOS systems. A long or float is a 4-byte entity, and a double consumes 8 bytes. When peeking and poking in memory, we normally wish to do this one byte at a time. Other pointer types will not allow for a 1-byte return or a 1-byte write, at least not in the direct manner char pointers do.

"But you said all pointers in small-memory model compilers for MS-DOS machines are 2-byte entities, and in large models, they have 4 bytes for storage!" That's right, but this applies only to the area set aside for the pointer to store an address. The number of bytes they return or access is fixed at one for chars, two for ints and unsigneds, four for floats and longs, and eight for doubles (again, assuming a typical MS-DOS implementation).

The following program (compiled with a small-memory model) will further explain char pointer alignment.

```
#include <iostream.h>
#include <stdlib.h>
int main()
{

    int far *x;
    char far *a;

    x = (int far *) 0xb8000000;
    a = (char far *) 0xb8000000;

    system("cls");

    cout << 'A' << endl << endl;

    cout << int(*a) << endl << *x << endl;

}
```

This program declares two far pointers. Pointer *x* is of type int, while *a* is of type char. Both pointers are given the address of the start of the VGA display buffer. The system()

function is used to call the CLS command that clears the display screen and resets the cursor to the upper left hand corner. The cout stream is accessed and prints an 'A' in the upper left corner of the screen followed by two newlines (endl).

The stream is accessed again to display the values in *a and in *x. Remember, both of these pointers have been given the same address. Both point to the first byte of screen memory, but a is of type char and x is of type int.

The expectation here is to display two values of 65, the first one being the cast value in *a, with the second value directly returned by *x. But that's not what happens! Instead, you get 65 on one line and 1857 on the other. The char pointer returned the correct value, but so did the int pointer with its 1857. How can this be? There can't be two values for the first byte in the screen buffer!

This is a true statement. However, the char pointer accesses memory in 1-byte quantities. A char can't represent more than one byte of data. The int pointer accesses data in 2-byte increments. The return from an int pointer is not a 1-byte quantity but a 2-byte value. Earlier, it was stated that the text screen buffer uses every other byte (even numbers and 0) for character display. The odd bytes are used to set the character attributes. In a normal screen, all of the odd bytes have a value of 7. Therefore, the value returned by the int pointer was the 2-byte combination of 65 and 7. ASCII 65 is the code for 'A'. The 7 is the attribute byte. However, the 2-byte coding for a numeric value of 1857 is, you guessed it, 65 and 7.

The char pointer returned a 1-byte value that was written to the screen as its integer equivalent of 65. This is the only value found in that single byte. The int pointer returned a 2-byte standard int value that was also written to the screen as its 2-byte integer equivalent of 1857. This can be explained mathematically in the following manner.

```
1857 % 256 = 65 // First Byte
1857 / 256 = 7 // Second Byte
```

The opposite event takes place when a poke operation is attempted with a pointer of type int. Assuming that x is a far pointer with the address of the VGA screen buffer and of type int, the following expression will cause a value of 65 ('A') to be written to the first byte in the buffer, but a 0 will also be written at the second byte.

```
*x = 65;
```

The first write is what we're looking for. The second definitely is not! The second byte (the odd one) is the attribute byte for the screen display. A value of 0 here causes the character at the first buffer byte to become invisible. The result for a full screen write of all characters 'A' is a blank screen if an int pointer is used for this purpose.

Think of pointers as returning one standard storage unit (SSU) of data or of writing one SSU. This applies regardless of the pointer type. However, the SSU for a char or void type is 1 byte. SSU size for all other data types is 2 or more bytes.

Far pointers specifically introduced into small-memory model programs work just as well for writing or poking data into memory. The following program demonstrates a poke operation using a far pointer.

```
int main()
{

    char far *a;

    a = (char far *) 0xb8000000;

    *a = 65;

}
```

This program writes an 'A' to the first byte in the VGA screen buffer and can be compiled by the small-memory model option. It should be mentioned that the large-model classification of compiler options offers advantages other than being able to address all memory. These advantages include the ability to handle large programs that will not compile using small-memory models. While it is usually preferable to remain within the boundaries of the small-memory model compilers wherever possible, source code size and content will dictate the model that is best suited for a particular program. In some cases, you may have to try both model classifications to see which compilation is best for a particular purpose. If you switch from one to the other, it will be necessary to change the source code slightly when pointer operations that use direct addresses are included. If you compile a program using the large-memory model, then recompilation with the small-memory model will require that pointers used for far memory access be declared *far* pointers. Going from a small- to a large-memory model is not nearly so tedious. In the large models, a pointer is a 4-byte entity by default. Any pointer that is declared *far* in the large model is unaffected by the modifier and is still allocated 4 bytes for address storage.

There are also other compiler options that are a combination of both large and small. For instance, the medium-memory model in the Borland C++ compiler defaults to far pointers for the code (program) segment, but the data segment defaults to near pointers. This means that the medium model is ideal for compiling C++ programs with a large amount of source code (larger than can be accommodated by the small-memory model) while still maintaining the efficiency of near pointers in the data segment. No far accesses into memory will be permitted without declaring far pointers for this purpose.

The opposite of the medium model is the compact-memory model. Using this option, the program segment is limited to near pointers, but all of memory can be accessed via the far pointer default in the data segment. For C++ programs with only a moderate amount of source code, this model is recommended, especially if many excursions into far memory are anticipated.

Summary

A pointer contains the address of an object in memory. If the address is specified directly as a numeric value, then the object at that address can be retrieved. This is a peek operation. If the address is assigned an object value, then the memory location is overwritten, which is a poke operation. Unintentional overwrites can be disastrous, but a poke is intentional and desirable (provided the programmer knows what he or she is doing).

Char pointers are an excellent choice for reading and writing memory locations in a standard fashion. Their 1-byte objects are responsible for this desirability. All other types of pointers may also be used for memory accessing, but one must always remember the SSU size of each type.

Large-memory model compilers automatically allocate 4 bytes of storage for all pointers. This allows excursions through all of a computer's memory (assuming typical maximum memory sizes). However, the large model compilers with their automatic far pointers create programs that are usually larger in size than those produced by small-memory model compilers. Execution speed with large model compilations is slowed, sometimes considerably.

Most popular C++ compilers for MS-DOS machines offer the advantage of declaring far pointers from within their small-memory model options. This provides full memory access while maintaining many of the advantages of the small-memory model attributes. Even with the small-memory model compilers, 4-byte pointers still take longer to execute than do their 2-byte counterparts. However, small-model programs that utilize both near (2-byte) and far pointers will execute faster than they would if compiled entirely with a large model.

One rule always applies: Initialize all pointers before using them. In every program example in this chapter, pointers were always initialized, given a memory address, before any reading or writing took place. When using far pointers, whether specifically declared from a small-memory model program or from a large model program, the full-memory capability can lead to very real dangers if uninitialized pointers are used to write memory. With far pointers, it is now possible to tap into your system's various interrupts. An unintentional poke into memory can bring about potential disaster. Always know where your pointers are directed.

Chapter 6

Pointers and Memory Allocation

A pointer must always point to something. This is the first rule of thumb when dealing with declared pointers and is called pointer *initialization*. All pointers must be assigned a memory address before usage, or they will address random memory locations that can wreck a program and even damage disk files.

In most previous program examples, pointers were assigned the memory addresses of other variables. In peek/poke operations, pointers were assigned the addresses of memory locations specifically for the purpose of reading a byte content or writing to a byte of storage.

There are many advantages to using pointers, but in most cases, we depend upon standard variables for safe areas that the pointers may reference. Char arrays are necessary for storing copied strings, but they must be sized to accommodate the largest string length. Wouldn't it be nice if a device were available to allocate memory based upon the size of the string to be copied, rather than on some size roughly determined by the programmer and oversized for the sake of avoiding an accidental memory overwrite.

Memory Allocation Functions

The two principal memory allocation functions that are part of the C++ function libraries are *malloc()* and *calloc()*. They both perform the same basic process of setting aside a safe area of memory to which data may be written, and these data blocks may be of any practical size. Both functions perform operations that check on memory availability, based on the memory block size requested. When a suitable segment of memory is located, a pointer to the address of the allocated block is returned by the function. The principal difference between malloc() and calloc() is that the latter clears all of the allocated memory, poking zeros into each byte. Malloc() simply allocates the memory without clearing the bytes. The value of each byte is whatever value was already contained there prior to the allocation.

Malloc()

The following program begins our discussion of pointers and memory allocation functions.

```
#include <string.h>
int main()
{

    char a[5][14];

    strcpy(a[0], "Charlotte");
    strcpy(a[1], "Scamp");
    strcpy(a[2], "Forget Me Not");
    strcpy(a[3], "Golf");
    strcpy(a[4], "Computer")

}
```

This program uses a two-dimensional char array sized to store up to five strings, each with a maximum length of 14 bytes, including the NULL terminator. The program allocates 70 bytes (5 * 14) for storage to the array. However, the total storage required for these five string constants is only 44 bytes. This means that 26 bytes are wasted when using the string constants in this program. The reason for the waste is the manner in which the array declaration must be made. The smallest value allowed in the second part of the subscript must be capable of containing the largest string. However, this large value applies to the other four string storage allocations within the array.

The following program is another example of wasted storage.

```
#include <iostream.h>
int main()
{

        int x;
        char a[5][256];

        for (x = 0; x < 5; ++x)
                cin >> a[x];

}
```

This example cannot use a pointer substitute, since no string constants are involved. The cin stream copies bytes retrieved from the keyboard into memory. This program assumes that the longest string will be composed of 255 typed characters and makes room for the NULL with the last. There is no way of knowing just what will be input, so an overly large string length must be assumed for the sake of safety.

However, we can conserve memory via the memory allocation functions and the addresses they return to pointers. The following program allocates storage for all strings input at the keyboard based on the length of any string.

```
#include <string.h>
#include <stdlib.h>
#include <iostream.h>
int main()
{

        char *a, b[256];

        cin >> b;

        a = malloc(strlen(b));

        strcpy(a, b)

}
```

The operation of this program is simple, because only two char types are declared. Variable *a* is a char pointer and *b* is a char array with a maximum storage capability of 256 characters including the NULL. The malloc() function returns a void. This is a generic pointer type that may be assigned to any other type of pointer without casting. In this program, the void pointer returned from malloc() is directly assigned to the char pointer.

The gets() function uses char array *b* as its storage device. This array can accept up to 255 characters without overwriting memory. The last character (256) is the NULL. The malloc() function is called, and it uses the length of the string already contained in *b* and returned by the strlen() function to determine how many bytes must be allocated. The strlen() function returns the total number of bytes in the string including the NULL. Therefore, malloc() will allocate just enough memory, no more and no less, to store the string in array *b*. Next, strcpy() is used to copy the string in *b* to the pointer location contained in *a*. This address was returned to *a* by the malloc() function.

Wait a minute! Didn't we just *copy* something to a pointer? Isn't this supposed to be taboo? Ordinarily, the answer is yes. Nothing should be copied to an uninitialized pointer. However, this pointer has been assigned the address of a block of memory that has been allocated especially for storage. Therefore, the pointer is initialized. This is a safe area guaranteed by the malloc() function. The strcpy() function treats *a* as it would a pointer to a char array. Before each copy, adequate storage is set aside at the address contained in *a*. If there is adequate storage, there is no reason why data cannot be copied into this block of memory. The argument to malloc() is the return from strlen(). This assures that the block is of adequate size. In reality, nothing is copied to the pointer. Rather, data are copied into the allocated memory block referenced by the pointer.

This program was simplified to the bare essentials for explanation purposes. The use of memory allocation functions *mandates* checking their returns for a NULL. These functions return NULL if the amount of memory requested is unavailable. If a NULL return is issued by the function, then the pointer value will be zero (NULL). If this test is not made and a NULL is returned, any attempt to write to the anticipated block of memory (which doesn't exist if the return is NULL) will result in a dangerous memory overwrite. The proper method of handling the operation carried out by the previous code is demonstrated by the following program.

```
#include <iostream.h>
#include <string.h>
#include <stdlib.h>
int main()
{

    char *a, b[256];
```

```
        cin >> b;

        a = malloc(strlen(b));

        if (a == NULL) {
            cout << "Out of Memory" << endl;
            exit(0);
        }
        else
            strcpy(a, b);
}
```

This can be shortened to the code that follows.

```
#include <string.h>
#include <stdlib.h>
#include <iostream.h>
int main()
{

    char *a, b[256];

    cin >> b;
    if ((a = malloc(strlen(b))) == NULL) {
        cout << "Out of Memory" << endl;
         exit(0);
    }
    else
        strcpy(a, b);

}
```

In both examples, the return value from malloc() is tested for a value of NULL, which is defined in the stdio.h header file. In most implementations, NULL is assigned a value of 0, but large-memory models require that the value be a long data type (0L).

When malloc() is called, a conditional test is performed on the value returned to the pointer. If this value is NULL, then the program displays an "Out of Memory" prompt and terminates execution. If the value returned by malloc() is other than 0, then the attempt was successful and this value becomes a pointer to the allocated block. When large blocks of memory are required, the large-memory model compiler versions may be required.

Imagine that you need to create a char array that will hold a very large string of, say,

60,000 characters. Don't try a declaration line like the one that follows.

```
char a[60000];
```

You would quickly find that this exceeds the size your compiler will accept. You may not be able to think of a reason why anyone would need an array of this size, but there are many. For instance, an entire block of characters from a word processor file could be stored in a single variable. The block could then be written or displayed by accessing the same variable, but you can't accomplish this through normal declarations. The following program shows how this amount of storage could be allocated to one variable unit.

```
#include <stdlib.h>
#include <iostream.h>
int main()
{

    char *a;

    if ((a = malloc(60000)) == NULL) {
        cout << "Out of Memory" << endl;
        exit();
    }

    /* Remainder of program ...... */
```

You now have a pointer that references a large block of memory for whatever purpose you need.

The memory allocation functions are certainly not limited to char values. Any pointer of any legal data type may contain the address of a malloc() assignment. The following program demonstrates this principle.

```
#include <stdlib.h>
#include <iostream.h>
int main()
{
    int *x, y;

    if ((x = malloc(400)) == NULL) {
        cout << "Out of memory" << endl;
        exit(0);
    }
}
```

```
        else
            for (y = 0; y <= 198; ++x)
                *(x + y) = 88;


    }
```

This program declares an int pointer and requires an explanation. In pre-ANSI C compilers, malloc() usually returned a pointer of type char. With the advent of ANSI C and C++, malloc() was changed to return a void pointer, one that is untyped. Such a pointer can be assigned directly to any other type of pointer without casting. A void pointer is generic, a pointer to any type.

The reason for the preference of char pointers for memory allocation lies in the fact that this data type utilizes 1-byte storage units. Therefore, 400-char SSUs can be stored in a memory block of 400 bytes. However, this program uses an int pointer to access the memory block of 400 bytes. Each assignment to $*x$ will result in a 2-byte write. Therefore, only 200 int values can be stored in the allocated memory block. If you try to write 400 integer values, thinking that there is enough allocated memory for this purpose, then you will overwrite the 400 bytes of memory that lie at the end of the block, which is very dangerous!

The *for* loop that loads the block (with a value of 88) counts from 0 to 198. Each time an int value is written, two of the 400 available bytes in the block are used. The argument to malloc() is expressed in bytes. However, the following construct deals in SSUs.

```
    *(x + y)
```

If $y = 0$, then $*x$ accesses the first two bytes of the block. However, $*(x + 1)$ does not access the second *byte* in the block. It accesses the second *SSU*. Since we are dealing with ints, the SSU is 2 bytes. Therefore, $*(x + 1)$ accesses the second SSU that is contained in the third and forth bytes in the block. The following mini-chart may help in picturing this concept.

```
    int *       (x + 0)  *(x + 1)  *(x + 2)  *(x + 3)  *(x + 4)
    Byte #       0 , 1     2 , 3     4 , 5     6 , 7     8,  9
```

The offset value [i.e., 2 in the expression $*(x + 2)$] can be thought of as half of the block byte position number being accessed. This is not too hard to remember, but different data types (float, long, double, etc) will also result in different SSUs.

While it has not been stated previously, the standard technique of specifying offsets to pointers, as in $*(x + 2)$, may also be expressed in subscripting brackets. Observe the assignment below.

```
*(x + 3) = 88;
```

This can also be expressed in the following manner.

```
x[3] = 88;
```

You don't often see expressions of this type involving declared pointers, the exception often being pointers that have been assigned the address of a block of allocated memory. In programs that use both arrays and pointers, the bracketed offset designations can become confusing. This is the reason for the availability of the more common *(x + 2) offsetting syntax that is often used with declared pointers. The two methods offer an expressiveness that tends to keep the two types separate in the mind of the programmer. To add to the possible confusion, offsets within arrays can also be expressed using the indirection operator.

```
#include <iostream.h>
int main()
{

        int x[40];

        *(x + 0) = 65;

        cout << char(*(x + 0)) << endl;

}
```

Arrays and pointers can often be treated as one and the same in many C++ operations, and these examples highlight that statement. However, the conventions that have evolved naturally since the C++ language was authored dictate the use of the indirection operator for memory access via pointers and the bracketed subscripts when dealing with declared arrays.

The following program shows a practical use for malloc() wherein the VGA screen is read and the contents saved in a memory block. The screen will then be cleared and the contents read back in again. Readers who are using a monochrome monitor should change the pointer address to 0xb0000000 for this program to work on their systems.

```
#include <iostream.h>
#include <stdlib.h>
#include <dos.h>
int main()
{
```

```
char far *a, *b;
int x;

 a = (char far *) 0xb8000000;

 if ((b = malloc(4000)) == NULL) {
      cout << "Out of memory" << endl;
      exit(0);
 }

 for (x = 0; x < 24; ++x)
      cout <<"Save the Screen" << endl;

 for (x = 0; x < 4000; ++x)
      *(b + x) = *(a + x);

 system("cls");
 sleep(5);

 for (x = 0; x < 4000; ++x)
      *(a + x) = *(b + x);


}
```

This program can be compiled using the small-memory model compiler option and is quite impressive even on the slower machines. A char far pointer, *a*, is given the address of the screen buffer. Char pointer, *b*, is assigned the address of the memory block allocated by malloc(). Note that the return from malloc() is tested for NULL. The first *for* loop is used to write a sentence to the screen and repeats it so the entire screen is filled. The next *for* loop reads the contents of the screen a byte at a time. As each byte is read from the screen buffer, it is copied to the memory block referenced by *b*. The copy is made on a byte-for-byte basis, resulting in the first byte from the screen, *(a + 0)*, being copied to the first byte in the block, *(b + 0)*. This continues until the 4000th byte from the screen is copied to the 4000th block byte. This completes the copy of the entire screen.

At this point in the execution chain, the screen is cleared by calling the MS-DOS CLS routine via the C++ system() function. The sleep() function is then called, which will produce a five-second pause. Without this function, the rewrite of the screen occurs so rapidly after screen clearing that you probably wouldn't be able to see the erasure. The sleep() function lets you plainly see that the screen has been cleared.

After five seconds, another *for* loop is executed that does the opposite of the previous loop. This time, the contents of the memory block are read back into the screen buffer. The copy takes place on a byte-for-byte basis, and all of the original screen information is rewritten in the blink of an eye.

This program could just as easily have transferred the contents to a disk file, but the process would have taken far longer due to the slower operation of mechanical devices. The playback of the disk information into the cleared screen would take as long. I have written several commercial software packages that have used routines similar to the one demonstrated by the last program. These programs contained many tutorial screens, and writing information to them in the usual fashion was too slow and would have created comprehension difficulties on the part of students. The solution was to download all screens to disk files. This was done outside of the tutorial program, proper. When I had all of the screens on disk, I included these files with the tutorial software. During a program run, several screens were loaded into memory blocks. This was done as soon as the program was executed and was part of the overhead time required for loading all information and before the on-screen run started. Then, when a screen was required, it was written directly from a memory block. The write took place almost instantly, and it was possible for the student to switch from one screen to another in a very short time, like flipping the pages of a book.

The following program shows a standard method of saving a screen to a disk file and assumes that the screen buffer already contains the information to be saved.

```
#include <iostream.h>
#include <fstream.h>
#include <stdlib.h>
int main()
{

    char far *a;
    int x;

    ofstream fp("screen1");

    if (!fp) {
        cout << "Error: Can't open file" << endl;
        exit(0);
    }

    a = (char far *) 0xb8000000;

    for (x = 0; x < 4000; ++x)
        fp.put(*a++);

}
```

This program opens a file using the C++ output file stream, *ofstream*. The char far pointer, *a*, is given the address of the VGA screen buffer. (Monochrome monitor users will want to change this address assignment to 0xb0000000.)

A *for* loop is entered and steps through each of the 4000 byte offsets in the buffer. While only the even bytes contain the character information, all bytes are read since the entire screen is to be saved. This means that any special text attributes will also be saved. Within the loop, the put() member function of the stream is used to write each byte to the disk file. You will notice that the pointer access is stepped by the increment operator *following* the pointer name. This means that the value in **a* will be returned to the function *prior* to the pointer being stepped to the next position. Here, we are actually changing the address in the pointer. We could also have written this statement in the following manner.

```
fp.put(*(a + x));
```

This method adds the value of *x* to the address in the pointer, the latter remaining fixed. Either method is acceptable, but the first increments the pointer address while the second uses the pointer address, unchanged, adding the offset to this value. Both result in the same assignments to the disk file.

Upon program termination, the file is closed and the disk contains a file named "screen1", loaded with all of the screen information. These data can be written back to the screen by using the program shown below.

```
#include <iostream.h>
#include <fstream.h>
#include <stdlib.h>
int main()
{

    char far *a, c;

    ifstream fp("screen1");

    if (!fp) {
        cout << "Cannot open disk file" << endl;
        exit(0);
    }

    a = (char far *) 0xb8000000;

    while (fp && fp.get(c))

    *a++ = c;


}
```

Each character is retrieved from the disk file and then is written to the screen. This process is repeated 4000 times until the entire screen has been written.

Each value returned to char *c* by the get() member function is assigned as the object at the screen buffer location accessed by *a*. The screen is rewritten, byte by byte. This will take some time (depending upon the type of microprocessor and the machine clock speed), and the lags may be very obvious to the screen viewer. The following program shows another method of retrieving this code from the disk. The process takes as long for recovery, but the display write is almost instantaneous.

```
#include <iostream.h>
#include fstream.h>
#include <stdlib.h>
#include <conio.h>
int main()
{

    int x, y;
    char far *a, *b, c;

    a = (char far *) 0xb8000000;

    if ((b = malloc(4000)) == NULL) {
        cout << "Out of memory" << endl;
        exit(0);
    }

    ifstream fp("screen1");

    if (!fp) {
        cout << "Error:Can't open file" << endl;
        exit(0);
    }

    y = 0;

    while (fp && fp.get(c))
    *(b + y++) = c;

    cout << "Press any key to see screen" << endl;

getch();

    for (x = 0; x < 4000; ++x)
        *a++ = *b++;

}
```

This program may seem to be complex to those new to C++, but it can be broken down into small, easy-to-understand modules.

Two char pointers are declared, far *a* and (near) *b*. The first is given the address of the VGA screen buffer. The second is handed the address of the start of 4000 bytes of memory cleared by malloc(). At this point, the file containing the screen information written by a previous program is opened. The *while* loop calls the get() stream member function that returns the contents of "screen1" in single-byte quantities to variable *c*. Within the *while* loop, the value in *c* is assigned to the byte accessed by pointer *b*. This byte and all others are within the 4000-byte block set aside by malloc(). Nothing is written to the screen by this action. Instead, the original screen contents stored in this disk file are written to the reserved block of 4000 bytes. This is a relatively slow process because each byte must be retrieved from the file and then written into memory. This was the same condition found in the previous program that wrote the screen directly from the disk file.

Once the memory block has been loaded, a prompt appears telling the user to press any key to write the screen. The getch() function is utilized here to halt program execution until a character is received from the keyboard. This character serves no purpose in this program other than to release the getch() execution halt.

When the key is pressed, a *for* loop is entered and the contents within the memory block are written directly to the screen. Pointer *b* returns the byte from the memory block that is written to the screen through access by far pointer *a*.

This program does not get the contents from disk file to screen any faster than did the previous program, but the time between actually starting and ending the write is tremendously fast. The time overhead comes from the necessity of loading the information from a disk file.

When you need several pages of information, load them all in at the same time. Once the screens have been copied to memory blocks, they may then be accessed almost instantaneously. From the user's point of view, it is far more pleasing to initialize and complete the long loading process during the initial call up or execution of the program. Of course, multiple pages will require more memory block allocations. The number of pages that can be loaded simultaneously will depend upon the amount of memory your machine has and also on the memory model compiler version. Large models are able to allocate more memory than can small models.

Calloc()

The malloc() function simply finds a free block in memory and then returns a pointer to it. Calloc() works in a similar fashion, except that it is more convenient when allocating memory for storage units of more than one byte. Also, calloc() clears all memory blocks as a part of its operation. This means that a block of 4000 bytes allocated by calloc() will return a pointer to a block whose bytes have been set to NULL (zero). The following program is similar to another example in this chapter but effectively demonstrates one of the advantages calloc() offers.

```
#include <iostream.h>
#include <stdlib.h>
int main()
{

    int *x, y;

    if ((x = calloc(400, 2)) == NULL {
        cout << "Out of memory" << endl;
        exit(0);

    }

    for (y = 0; y < 400; ++y)
        *(x + y) = 88;

}
```

Referring to the earlier program that assigned the address of a 400-byte memory block to an int pointer, you will remember that int values numbering a maximum of 200 were all that could be written to the block, because an int value requires 2 bytes of storage. In this example, another int pointer is used. Calloc() is called in the following format.

```
calloc(storage_units, unit_size)
```

The arguments express the number of storage units and the unit size. Therefore, the usage of calloc() in this program does not mean that a block of 400 bytes is allocated. Rather, the block is 800 bytes long. The number of storage units is 400, but the size of each storage unit is 2 bytes. Therefore, 400 * 2 = 800 bytes. This program can safely address 0 to 399 units in this block without overwriting memory. This means that *(x + 399) will access the 799th and 800th bytes in the allocated block. But, we don't have to worry about this aspect of storage after an allocation for the desired number of storage units has been made. Malloc() requires arguments in the form of bytes. Arguments to calloc() deal with storage units.

Throughout this book, I have stressed that stated storage sizes for various data types apply only to *most MS-DOS implementations*. This is important, because C++ offers excellent portability and is often used on minicomputers and very large systems. On these other types of machines, a standard int type may be allocated 4 bytes of storage, a long, 8 bytes, etc. Storage allocations for all data types in C++ are relative and based on the architecture of the machine and many other factors.

The built-in argument protocol of calloc() allows for portability to many other types of machines if the arguments are stated correctly. In the previous program, calloc() was used in the following form.

```
calloc(400, 2)
```

The desire here was to set aside 400 storage units for int values, an int requiring 2 bytes of storage. This is all well and good when dealing with an MS-DOS machine, but suppose the program containing this use of calloc() is to be ported to many other types of computers. There is no portability, because other machines may have different sizes (other than 2 bytes) for int values.

The way to maintain portability is to test the size of storage on the machine that will run the software; that is, base the allocation on the storage size that is tested while the program is running. How is that done?

Simple! Call the sizeof() operator, which has been used sparingly in some of the program examples in this text. This operator returns the size (in bytes) of any variable as well as the size of any data type specified.

```
sizeof(int)
```

This use will return the size of an int data type. Here, *int* is a keyword that can be read directly by the function. If this function were executed on an MS-DOS machine, sizeof() would return a value of 2, but on a mainframe, it might return 4 or more bytes.

With this in mind, calloc() could have been used in the previous program in this manner.

```
calloc(400, sizeof(int));
```

Such usage would insure that the correct number of bytes were set aside for the storage of 400 int data types, regardless of the amount of storage allocated to int data types. The calloc() function is already portable. You should make certain that your arguments to it and other such functions are equally portable.

There is nothing magic about the way calloc() performs its task. In fact, it simply calls malloc() as a part of its internal coding, then it assigns each allocated byte a value of zero. The following is an example of how malloc() can be called to exhibit the same portability as calloc().

```
malloc(400 * sizeof(int))
```

The argument to malloc() is a mathematical expression. The number of bytes is expressed as storage units multiplied by the size of the individual unit. This is exactly what calloc() does within its source code structure. The only difference in these two functions is that when malloc() is used in this manner, it does not reset all allocated bytes to NULL.

When an allocated block of memory is no longer needed, it should be freed up for later program allocation requests. This assumes that the program will continue to run long after the point in the execution chain where the allocated block is no longer needed. To free a block of memory that was allocated with either malloc() or calloc(), use the free() function in the following manner.

```
free(ptr)
```

In this example, *ptr* is the pointer to the block of allocated memory.

A More Modern Method of Memory Allocation

The use of memory allocation functions such as malloc() and calloc() is a holdover from the C and ANSI C programming languages from which C++ was derived. While these functions will still be used as outlined in this chapter, C++ offers an easier and more expressive means of allocation that doesn't involve traditional functions at all.

New and Delete

In ANSI C, dynamic memory allocation/deallocation is accomplished through the use of the UNIX library functions, such as malloc() and free(), or through specialized functions that are relevant to one type of compiler only and thus not portable. The malloc() function sets aside blocks of memory, while free() is used to release these allocated blocks. C++ defines a new method of performing dynamic memory allocation using the *new* and *delete* operators.

The following example illustrates a method of memory allocation using the malloc() function. Deallocation is accomplished with the free() function.

```
#include <iostream.h>
#include <stdlib.h>
int main()
{

    int *ip;

    ip = (int *) malloc(sizeof(int));
    *ip = 12126;

    cout << *ip << endl;
```

```
                    free(ip);


        }
```

In C++, the *new* operator can be used to completely replace malloc(), while the *delete* operator takes the place of free(). Using C++ conventions, the previous program can be written as follows.

```
        #include <iostream.h>
        int main()
        {

            int *ip;

            ip = new int;// return pointer to block
            *ip = 12126;// assign object value

            cout << *ip << endl;// display pointer value

            delete ip;// free allocated memory

        }
```

The C++ method using the *new* and *delete* operators is a simpler and far more direct approach to allocating and freeing up memory for the pointer.

You cannot use a constant value directly with the *new* operator, as attempted by the code fragment below.

```
        c = new 512;//Incorrect
```

Here, the intent is to set aside 512 bytes of data referenced by the pointer, *c.* Although it is easy to accomplish this with the *new* operator, the above example is incorrect and is shown because it represents some of the flawed attempts made by persons first learning C++.

The following program continues this discussion.

```
        #include <iostream.h>
        #include <stdlib.h>
        int main()
        {

            char *c;

            c = (char *) malloc(512);
```

```
        cin >> c;

        cout << c << endl;

        free(c);

    }
```

To accomplish the same thing using the *new* and *delete* operators and eliminating the memory allocation/deallocation functions along with their considerable overhead, use the following program.

```
#include <iostream.h>
void main(void)
{
        char *c;

        c = new char[512]; //obtain 512 char block
        cin >> c;
        cout << c << endl;

        delete c;

}
```

This method of memory allocation is a vast improvement, both in conservation of program memory and in ease of use.

Note that pointer *c* is assigned a value of

```
new char[512]
```

This means that total memory allocation will be

```
512 X char
```

or 512 times the number of bytes allocated to a char data type. In most MS-DOS applications, a char is allocated 1 byte of storage, so a total of 512 bytes will be allocated. In contrast, if the assignment line had been written as

```
c = new int[512]
```

then a total of 1024 bytes (512 * 2) would be allocated, assuming that 2 bytes are reserved for int data types. This format provides a definite programming advantage in that the sizeof() operator is not necessary to allocate the correct amount of storage, and portability is still maintained across different systems/compilers.

If *new* cannot allocate the requested amount of memory, its return value is NULL. This action mirrors malloc(), which also returns NULL when an allocation error occurs. The above examples are as simple as possible and do not include checks for the NULL return. However, good programming practice absolutely requires such checks to avoid memory overwrites. A simple check can be made using an *if* statement construct as shown below.

```
if ((c = new char[512]) == NULL)
        exit(0);
```

Because the *new* and *delete* operators can take the place of malloc() and free() in the standard function set, and because these operators offer a simpler and more direct approach, it makes sense to use them exclusively.

In general, it's best to use one form of memory allocation or the other. The UNIX memory allocation functions [malloc(), free(), calloc()] should not be used along with the *new* and *delete* operators. Trying to use both dynamic management systems can lead to all sorts of problems and inconsistencies. Memory allocated by *new* cannot be released by free(). Likewise, memory allocated by malloc() cannot be released by the *delete* operator.

The *new* operator will always return a pointer of the correct type without this type being specified by the programmer. For example:

```
int *x;
x = new int[14];
```

Here, *new* will return a pointer of type int, because the operand (*x*) is an int type. It is unnecessary to cast the pointer to the correct type. This is one of the major advantages of a memory allocation *operator* when compared to a function that accomplishes a similar operation.

The *new* and *delete* operators may be used to create and destroy multidimensional arrays shown in the code fragment that follows.

```
int *i;
i = new int[2][34];//create array

/* array is assigned here
        . . . . . . . . . . . . . . . .
```

```
. . . . . . . . . . . . . . .
. . . . . . . . . . . . . .
                                                    */
delete i; // destroy array
```

In this example, an array of 68 ints (two-dimensional) is created, setting aside a total of 136 bytes (assuming 2-byte integers). There are some restrictions on this usage, in that the first dimension in the array may be any valid expression, but the remaining dimension(s) must always be an int constant. For example, the expression

```
x = 10;
i = new int[x][34];
```

is perfectly valid. However,

```
x = 10;
i = new int[2][x];
```

is not, because all but the first dimension of an array must be expressed as an int constant. In every case, the *new* operator returns a pointer to the *first* element in the array. Also, *new* does not automatically initialize any memory objects it creates. The contents of a memory block allocated by *new* using the methods discussed to this point are meaningless until initialized within the program.

The *new* and *delete* operators serve a very useful purpose in taking the place of the UNIX functions for allocation of blocks of memory. However, these operators were especially designed for an object-oriented environment where objects must be created and later destroyed. When *new* is used to allocate memory for any object other than an array, an optional initializer may be used as shown below.

```
char *c;
int *x;
double *d;

c = new char('B');
x = new int(0);
d = new double(3.14159);
```

Three pointers are declared of type char, int, and double, respectively. When the *new* operator is invoked to allocate storage for each of these, the optional initializer is used. This initializes the pointers and writes the argument object to the memory block allocated. The initializer values are contained in parentheses and must match or have the capability of being cast to the type specified. For instance, if the initializer value for the double pointer was specified as 3, this would be cast to 3.0000000, while an initializer value to the int pointer of 6.75192 would be cast to the int value of 6. If the initializer value cannot be converted to the proper type, then initialization does not take place and the object is garbage.

Objects created by the *new* operator exist until they are destroyed by the *delete* operator or until the program ends. The *delete* operator is the only means of freeing memory allocated by *new* while execution is taking place. Failing to release memory allocated by *new* that is no longer needed is a poor programming practice that may leave insufficient memory for other applications. Even though program termination will automatically free all memory allocated by *new*, it is still good programming practice to release any allocated memory before the program ends. The free() function will have no effect on releasing these blocks. Conversely, you cannot free memory allocated by malloc() by using the *delete* operator.

The *delete* operator can be used for purposes other than freeing memory allocated by *new*. For instance, it can be used to erase the address in a pointer without actually deleting the variable. The following program shows a simple example of this operation.

```
#include <iostream.h>
int main()
{

    char *a, *b;

    b = "Language";
    a = b;

    cout << a << endl;

    delete a;

    cout << a << endl;

}
```

Char pointers *a* and *b* are declared and pointer *b* is assigned the address of the string constant, "Language". Next, pointer *a* is assigned the address in pointer *b*. Both pointers now contain the address of the first byte in "Language". Using cout, the object referenced by pointer *a* ("Language") is displayed on the screen. Next, the *delete* operator is used to destroy the address in pointer *a*. The next line displays the object referenced by *a* again, but this results in garbage being written to the screen because the address in pointer *a* has been destroyed.

One decided advantage of using *new* and *delete* for memory allocation/destruction is slightly faster execution time, because we are dealing with built-in operators as opposed to functions. However, compilation times for programs using *new* and *delete* will be slightly slower than those that use the UNIX memory functions. This is a fair trade-off, as execution time should be the most important of the two.

Summary

When a pointer is assigned the address of an allocated block of memory, we can say that it has been initialized and, in a manner of speaking, has been *sized* to the number of bytes in the storage area. It is then safe to copy objects to this memory block using the pointer for access. The pointer may be treated as an array of the same size as the memory block the pointer addresses.

Both malloc() and calloc() will return a NULL value if the amount of memory requested cannot be allocated. Any program that uses either of these functions must test their returns for the NULL. If you assume that the storage space is available and it turns out that it isn't, then you will overwrite memory.

The C++ standard requires that malloc() and calloc() return pointers of type void. This means that the return address value can be assigned to any legal pointer data type. Casting is unnecessary.

Through the use of C++ pointers and the memory allocation functions, it is convenient to perform block reads and writes. These were demonstrated in this chapter by programs that read, wrote and rewrote the monitor screen. Such operations are certainly not limited to visual display screens and may be used to read and write any block of memory anywhere in the system. The reason for the screen buffer examples is that the memory writes can actually be seen, which is more expressive from a tutorial standpoint.

The *new* and *delete* operators provide a direct and expressive method of allocating and freeing memory. In most instances, C++ programmers will opt to use these instead of the UNIX memory allocation functions. Once a block of memory has been allocated by either *new* or malloc(), it is manipulated in exactly the same manner. In both instances, an address is returned to a pointer that names the start of the allocated block of memory. If the *new* operator cannot allocate the requested amount of memory, then a NULL return is handed to the pointer.

Chapter 7

Pointers and C++ Functions

It has already been established that arguments are passed to and from functions by value. It is not possible to change the value of a calling program variable within a function unless we have the address of a variable in the calling program. C++ functions have the capability of returning values that can be, in turn, assigned to variables within the calling program. However, through pointer operations, we can write specialized functions that will return a value to the calling program and change the values in other variables whose memory addresses are handed to the function. In this manner, it is possible to write a function that, figuratively, returns many values in a single operation. While pointers are indispensable throughout all phases of C++ programming, their capabilities yield high-powered program performance especially when dealing with programmed functions.

The direct programming of pointers gives C++ its power, expressiveness, and authority. It is also the pointer that has vaulted C++ to the top of the list of languages most desirable for software development.

The following program incorporates a special function to return the square of a value passed to it. This is a useless function for any but tutorial purposes, but as the discussion continues, other examples will be presented that provide some practical application.

```
#include <iostream.h>
int square(int);
int main()
{

    int x, y;

    x = 8;
    y = 11;

    x = square(x);
    y = square(y);

    cout << x < "" << y << endl;

}
int square(int a)
{

    return(a * a);

}
```

The square() function is passed a value from the calling program. This value is assigned to *a*, a variable that is internal to the function. The function return value is *a* * *a*, or the square of the passed value. This program will display the following values.

```
64121
```

Under main(), the square() function is called twice, because it is necessary to obtain the square of two different values. It is not possible for a C++ function to directly return two values. In this example, the function *equates* to the square of its passed value.

This next example shows how a similar function can accept the value of a calling variable *and* the memory address of another. The passed value is returned by the function, just as in the example above. However, the address is used to reassign the value in another variable to its square. The result is a function that returns a square value in the normal manner and rewrites one via a pointer.

```
#include <iostream.h>
int square(int, int *);
int main()
{

    int x, y;

    x = 8;
    y = 11;

    x = square(x, &y);

    cout << x << "" << y << endl;

}
int square(int a, int *b)
{

    *b = *b * *b; /* rewrite memory */
    return(a * a);/* return square */

}
```

This program will also display 64 and 121 on the screen, but the function was called only once, which results in a faster program run. In the function, *a* is an auto variable of type int, but *b* is a pointer of type int. The memory address of *y* in the calling program was passed to the function. The value of this address was assigned to pointer *b* in the function. The following expression will look a bit weird at first because of the number of asterisks.

```
*b = *b * *b;
```

The first two asterisks are indirection operators accessing the object at the address passed to the pointer. The third asterisk is the multiplicative operator, while the fourth is another indirection operator. If *b* were a standard (auto) variable, then this line would have been written in the following manner.

```
b = b * b;
```

The use of a single symbol to name several operators that perform differently in C++ is a very good reason to stick to established source code formatting conventions. All arithmetic operators should be separated from their variable names by a space.

```
x = a * b;
```

This expression is far easier to decipher than the one that follows.

```
x=a*b;
```

The multiplication of pointer *b* could also be written in C++ shorthand.

```
*b *= *b;
```

This means the same as the following expression.

```
*b = *b * *b;
```

Either way, there are still a lot of asterisks. But, suppose these examples did not adhere to the source code formatting conventions. We might end up with the following glob of source code.

```
*b=*b**b;
```

Alternately, consider the previous shorthand method, now bastardized by poor program formatting.

```
*b*=*b;
```

I have observed that, as ANSI C and C++ grow in popularity, there has been a breakdown in the standardized formatting conventions. Even many of the commercial references that accompany C++ compilers are sloppily formatted. This is not elitism on my part but an appeal. The writing of sloppy source code, regardless of the fact that it compiles and runs properly, is a detriment to newcomers learning this language. Also, it's getting harder for those of us who are supposed to know the language to decipher some of the garbled programs we see.

The example of a function returning a value, supposedly for assignment to another variable in the calling program, and changing the value of another calling program variable is not especially unique. However, this type of operation is more likely to be handled in a manner whereby two address values are sent to the function that returns a void value. The following code example demonstrates this.

```
#include <iostream.h>
void square(int *, int *);
int main()
{

    int x, y;

    x = 8;
    y = 11;

    square(&x, &y);

    cout << x << "" << y << endl;

}
void square(int *a, int *b)
{

    *a *= *a;
    *b *= *b;

}
```

The same result is had within the calling program, and the function source code is more typical of what one might expect.

In all of these examples, the function expected a specific number of arguments, and had to be passed this same number to prevent an error, but what about functions that accept a varying number of arguments? A good example is printf(), which is a part of the standard I/O stream. This function is used, seemingly, in different formats including those that follow.

```
printf("hello, world\n");
printf("%s\n", "hello, world");
printf("%d\n", x);
printf("%d%c\n", x, y);
```

How is this apparent bevy of arguments handled? The following program begins a discussion that will answer part of this question.

```
#include <stdio.h>
void newprint(char *, int, ...);
int main()
{

    int x, y;

    x = 17;
    y = 134;

    newprint("%d%d", x, y);

}
void newprint(char *str, int args, ...)
{

    printf("%s\n%d", str, args);
}
```

This program declares and assigns two int variables and then calls a new function, arbitrarily named newprint(). The arguments to newprint() are handled in the same manner that would apply if a similar call to printf() were involved. The newprint() function source code at the bottom of the calling program declares only two arguments in its parentheses, *str* and *args*. The ellipses (...) indicate to the compiler that the function may have any number of arguments following the char string and the int. The first argument is declared a char pointer, the second is an int. This is a test program purely for discussion purposes, so our first job is to see what the two arguments yield. We'll use the standard printf() function to display the values of the two arguments. The screen will display the following.

```
%d%d
17
```

This means that *str* points to the string that was enclosed in quotation marks within the original call to newprint(). A quoted constant in C++ actually returns the address of that constant in memory. Therefore, *str* points to the string constant "%d %d". The *args* variable is displayed as 17, the value of the first variable argument to newprint(). However, you will recall that two variable arguments were provided. Only one is displayed. The reason for this is that our printf() function within newprint() called only for one int argument in its format control string. However, *args* is only a single argument, so what do we do?

Though this program doesn't show it, the address assigned to *args* references both variable arguments originally made to newprint(). For now, we will say that the address of *args* references a block of memory that contains all of the values handed to newprint() during the initial call. The first two bytes contain the value in *x* (17) from the calling program. The second two bytes contain the value in *y*, 134. These values are aligned sequentially at the start of storage reserved for *args*. Incidentally, this storage was set aside automatically by the calling program when the newprint() function was invoked. Without going into laborious detail, this is the manner in which C++ handles function calls.

The following program reveals more about this discussion.

```
#include <stdio.h>
void newprint(char *, int, ...);
int main()
{

    int x, y;

    x = 17;
    y = 134;

    newprint("%d%d", x, y);

}
void newprint(char *str, int args, ...)
{

    int *ptr;

    ptr = &args;

    printf("%s\n%d\n%d\n", str, *ptr, *(ptr + 1));

}
```

This program will display the following on the monitor.

```
%d%d
17
134
```

This is what we are looking for. The big change in the function source code is in the way *ptr* is used. This is a pointer of type int that has been declared within the function. It was stated earlier that the address of int variable *args* references all of the second argument group passed to newprint(). The first argument group is the formatting string enclosed in quotes, so the storage address of *args* is the place to begin. Pointer *ptr* is given the address of *args* via the address-of operator. Now, *ptr* contains the object value of the first argument to newprint() (after the format string), and *(ptr + 1)* contains the second.

The arguments are changed slightly in the example that follows.

```
#include <stdio.h>
#include <string.h>
void newprint(char *, int, ...);
int main()
{

    int x, y;
    char a[20];

    x = 17;
    y = 134;

    strcpy(a, "Today");

    newprint("%d%d%s", x, y, a);

}
void newprint(char *str, int args, ...)
{
    int *ptr;
    ptr = &args;

    printf("%s\n%d\n%d\n%s", str, *ptr, *(ptr + 1), *(ptr +
2));

}
```

This produces the following monitor display.

```
%d%d%s
17
134
Today
```

Again, *ptr* returns the two bytes that equate to decimal 17; *(ptr + 1)* gives us 134, and *(ptr + 3)* returns the address of the storage location of "Today". In short, the storage address starting at the address of variable *args* forms a memory *chain* of actual values and/or addresses of strings.

Of course, we are cheating a bit, as the supposed purpose of newprint() is to replace the printf() function found in C++. Since newprint() calls printf(), this new function doesn't really take its place. The purpose of this discussion is to illustrate argument alignment in function calls, but to further this practicum, I will explain the workings of printf() in a little more detail as it expands on the subject of pointers.

The format string in printf() is the controlling element for reading the second argument grouping content. First, remember that if we want to print the letter 'C' on the screen, this letter does not reside, as a letter or character, anywhere in memory. It is stored, as are all data, as a numeric value. The ASCII value of 'C' is 67 decimal.

The printf() source code is long and complex because the function has to read the contents of the format control string, and access memory for the type of data specified, and then build up a character string accordingly. If the first element in the control string is a %d, the printf() source code instructs the function to access *ptr* (using the preceding example as a reference) or *(ptr + 0)*, if you prefer, and retrieve an int value. If the contents of the first two bytes addressed by the pointer are 17 and 0, this means that the numeric value equal to 17D is to be displayed as a decimal integer. However, we are writing to the screen, so we can't simply poke in a value of 17 at a character location. Instead, printf() has to place the character '1' followed by the character '7' in the display string it is building internally. The single number 17 is represented as two characters, a '1' and a '7'. The '1' is represented by ASCII 49 and the '7' by ASCII 55. Therefore, the values that must be poked into the display screen buffer to represent numeric 17 are 49 and 55. This is a long conversion from 17 and 0, the 2-byte storage code for the number, 17. This process applies to all other numeric values as well, with the larger numbers requiring a larger number of characters to represent them.

After the first two characters representing numeric 17D are placed at the front of the display string being built by the function, the format control string is read again, starting at a point just following the %d. Assume the next read yields a space. This signals no special memory access code, so it is simply displayed as the whitespace character that is printed when the keyboard space bar is pressed. The space character has a value of ASCII 32, so this value is added to the screen display string that now appears as follows.

```
49  55  32
```

The next format string read yields another %d. This alerts printf() to go to the next pointer position, *(ptr + 1)* and retrieve two bytes of integer data. The value returned goes through the same conversion process previously discussed. We'll assume the retrieved integer value is 28, which yields an ASCII character value of 50 and 56. The screen string construct in printf() now reads as follows.

```
49 55 32 50 56
```

Again, printf() goes back to the remainder of its format string. Let's assume that it next discovers another whitespace character. This character signals no special code, as does %d, for example, so the character is to be displayed as a space on the screen. The ASCII code for a space is 32. See how the character string has grown.

```
49 55 32 50 56 32
```

Once again, the format string is read, and this time a %s pops up. This signals a string value and printf() goes to the next argument vector of *(ptr + 2). Here, it looks for an address of a string, a pointer. It accesses that address location from the two bytes used by the pointer for storage (assuming that a small-memory model compiler defaulting to 2-byte pointers is used) and copies the numeric byte content to the end of the screen string it is building. If we assume the string content is "ABC", then 65, 66, and 67 are copied to the internal screen display string. The string has grown considerably.

```
49 55 32 50 56 32 65 66 67
```

Assuming that this is the end of the format control string, printf() is now ready to dump these contents. The following program should be familiar as it pokes bytes to the VGA screen buffer.

```
int main()
{
    char far *a, s[10];
    int x, y;

    a = (char far *) 0xb8000000;

    s[0] = 49;
    s[1] = 55;
    s[2] = 32;
    s[3] = 50;
    s[4] = 56;
    s[5] = 32;
    s[6] = 65;
```

```
            s[7] = 66;
            s[8] = 67;

            y = 0;

    /* Access every other byte in buffer */

            for (x = 0; x < 18; x += 2)
                *(a + x) = s[y++];

    }
```

This program will display the following string on the monitor.

```
    17 28 ABC
```

This has been a laborious process and doesn't even begin to reveal all of the complex workings of printf(). This explanation has been a brief and technically symbolic representation of the processes that a function like printf() must go through to deliver the screen output that we take for granted. This discussion has also revealed how a function can be written to handle an indeterminate amount of passed argument values. Without pointers, such operations would not be available to the programmer.

The concepts explained lead to other possibilities, such as functions that will perform mathematical operations on any number of arguments. The add() function is demonstrated by the following program.

```
            #include <iostream.h>
            int add(int, ...);
            int main()
            {

                int a, b, c, d, e, f;

                a = 12;
                b = 4;
                c = 8;
                d = 234;

                e = add(4, a, b, c, d);
                f = add(3, b, c, d);
```

```
                cout << e << endl << f << endl;

        }
        int add(int args, ...)
        {

                int tot, x, y, *ptr;

                ptr = &args;
                y = *ptr++;
                tot = 0;

                for (x = 0; x < y; ++x)
                      tot += *ptr++;

                return(tot);

        }
```

This program assigns values to four int variables and then calls add() two times in order to return the total of all its arguments to variables *e* and *f.* The following numeric values are displayed on the monitor.

```
        258
        246
```

The add() function accepts any number of integer arguments, but the first argument *must* state the number of arguments passed. The first call to add() uses four values to be added, so the first argument is 4. The second call uses a first argument of 3 to add the three values in the variable arguments that follow.

There is no format string in this function, but none is needed because the first argument is all that is necessary to effect the add operation. The only argument shown as being passed to add() is named *args* and resides within the body of the function. As before, *args* is the start of memory where all arguments to add() have been placed. The declared pointer is given the address of *args* and the first value is extracted. The following expression does two things.

```
        y = *ptr++;
```

The object value at the address contained within the pointer is returned to *y,* then the pointer address is incremented by one SSU, in this case, 2 bytes. The value in y is the first argument to add(). On the first call to this function, y is equal to 4, which is the total number of arguments to be added by the function. Another internal variable, *tot*, is assigned an initial value of 0. This is the variable that will contain the added totals.

Next, a *for* loop is entered that increments x from a value of 0 to y *minus 1*.Remember, y contains the number of arguments to be added. Counting from 0 to y - *1* will cause the loop to cycle the number of times in y. The loop count begins at 0, not 1. Assuming four arguments to be added, looping from 0 to 3 (y - *1*) will yield four loop cycles.

Pointer *ptr* has been incremented to the next data position during the object assignment to y and before the loop is entered. On the first pass of the loop, **(ptr + 1)* is accessed for a return value of 12 (the value of the passed argument in variable *a* from the calling program). The pointer is actually advanced by the increment operator, but **(ptr + 1)* is another way of expressing its relative position. The value of 12 is added to the current value in *tot*, which is 0. On the next pass, **(ptr + 2)* is accessed and added to the current value in *tot*. This variable is now equal to 16 (12 + 4). On the next pass, the 8 is added and then 234. The loop times out because it has cycled four times. The value in *tot* is now equal to the sum of the four arguments. This value is returned to the calling program, where it is assigned to *e*.

The next call to add() contains only three values to be added, so the first argument is three. The same operations begin again, except that the loop will cycle only three times due to the new value in y. This time, the total of the three arguments to add() will be returned.

Pointers to Functions

A C++ function is not a variable, but you can declare pointers to functions that can then be used in a manner in which other pointers are used, such as placing them in arrays, passing them to other functions, etc. One rarely sees a pointer to a function, but this technique can sometimes be used to advantage, such as in purposely hiding the intent of a program. Such a pointer tends to obscure the name and source code of that function. Muddying the waters is not a normal C++ programming purpose, but with the security placed on software these days, intentional misdirection seems to be growing.

The following program demonstrates the basic techniques of declaring a pointer to a function.

```
#include <iostream.h>
#include <string.h>
int hide(char *, int(*)(char *));
int length(char *);

int main()
```

```
        {

                int x;
                char *a = "Computer";

                x = hide(a, length);


                cout << x << endl;

        }
        int hide(char *c, int (*spider) (char *c))
        {

                return((*spider) (c));

        }
        int length(char *s)
        {

                int x = 0;

                while (*s++)
                        ++x;

                return(x);

        }
```

This process may look a little ridiculous, but it effectively demonstrates a pointer to a function. In this case, the function in question is length(), which returns the length of a string argument as an int in the same fashion that the intrinsic strlen() function does.

Within the calling program, the arbitrarily named hide() function is invoked. It requires two arguments, a char pointer and a function name. In this usage, *length* without parentheses is the address of the length() function. Just as the name of an array without the subscripting brackets is a pointer to the memory location of the array, a C++ function without the parentheses is a pointer to the memory location of that function.

Within hide(), the address of *a* is assigned to char **c*, and the address of *length* is passed to a pointer to this function arbitrarily named *spider*. The declaration of this entity within the function is shown below.

```
int (*spider) (char *c)
```

This states that **spider* is a pointer to a function that returns an int value, and char **c* is the argument to the function. The expression, *(*spider)* may be used exactly as you would length().

The following expression

```
return((*spider) (c));
```

means exactly the same thing as the one below.

```
return(length(c));
```

*(spider) (c) points to the storage address set aside for length() when it is declared within the program.

Functions Returning Pointers

It was shown how pointer arguments to functions can be used to alter values in the calling program. In such cases, no pointer values were returned from the function. The address value passed to the function was used for accessing a variable's address to make changes in memory. These discussions involve functions that return pointers to the calling program.

The following program calls a function that returns a *pointer* of type char.

```
#include <iostream.h>
#include <string.h>
char *combine(char *, char *);
int main()
{

    char a[10], b[10], *p;

    strcpy(a, "horse");
    strcpy(b, "fly");

    p = combine(a, b);

    cout << p << endl;
}
char *combine(char *s, char *t)
{
```

```
int x, y;
char r[100];

strcpy(r, s);
y = strlen(r);

for (x = y; *t != '\0'; ++x)
    r[x] = *t++;

r[x] = '\0';

return(r);

}
```

This program will display the following string on the monitor.

```
horsefly
```

The combine() function is nothing more than a version of strcat() that returns a pointer to the combined string and doesn't alter the value of any of its argument objects.

The program declares two char arrays, a char pointer. The *combine() function has been prototyped as one that returns a char pointer and accepts two char pointers as its arguments. Two string constants, "horse" and "fly", are copied to the two arrays. Next, combine() is called in the following format.

```
p = combine(a, b);
```

In this usage, *p* is a pointer of type char. Therefore, it must be handed the address of a char-type object. This means that the return from combine() must be a char pointer (or cast to a char * type).

Within the function source code, combine() is declared for a char * return by the opening line.

```
char *combine(char *s, char *t);
```

On return, this function will equate to a char pointer.

Within the function body, *x* and *y* are declared ints, and *r* is declared a char array with 100 bytes for storage. The subscript value need only be adequate to store the strings of *s* and *t* combined.

The strcpy() function is called to copy the string pointed to by *s* into *r*. Next, strlen() returns the number of characters in *r* and assigns this returned int value to *y*. A *for* loop is entered that assigns *x* a starting value of *y*. Since *y* is equal to the number of bytes in *r*, and *r* presently holds the contents of the string pointed to by *s*, this means that *x* will start its count at a value that is equal to the position of the NULL byte in *r*. This occurs because *x* is assigned an initial loop value of *y*, the latter being equal to 5.

To put it another way, the string pointed to by argument *s* has been copied into the *r* array. The end of this string is terminated by a NULL. The strlen() function returns the number of characters in *r*. We know that *s* points to "horse", a string containing five characters. When "horse" is copied into *r*, strlen(r) returns a value of 5. The character in *r* at the fifth offset (*r[5]*) is the NULL.

When the loop starts cycling, the initial value in *x* is 5. On the first pass, the NULL byte in *r* is overwritten by the first byte referenced by *t*, as shown below.

```
r[x] = *t++;
```

Pointer *t* is incremented by 1, and the loop cycles again. On the next pass, *x* is equal to 6, so byte *i[6]* receives the next character in **t*.

On each pass of the loop, the exit clause is tested.

```
*t != '\0'
```

Many programmers think that the second expression in a *for* loop must set the maximum value (or minimum value in negative-going loops) for the loop variable, in this case, *x*. This is not true! This portion of the loop statement is an exit clause, and may contain any legal expression. In this example, the loop will terminate when **t* is equal to NULL or '\0'. Each time *r[x] = *t++* is executed within the loop, pointer *t* is incremented. Before another loop cycle, the expression **t != \0'* is evaluated. When the end of the string referenced by *t* is reached, the loop will be exited.

Since we know that *t* points to "fly", we also know that the loop will cycle three times. After the third pass, the exit clause brings about a loop exit. However, the loop variable has already been incremented in readiness for the next pass. Even though this pass never came about, *x* is set to the next logical byte in *r*.

Since the termination of the loop occurred when the NULL character referenced by *t* was encountered, this NULL was never written to the end of *r*. Therefore, the contents of *r* encompass a series of discrete characters and not a string. A NULL terminator is required to make a string, so the contents of *r* are made into an official C++ string by the following assignment.

```
r[x] = '\0';
```

This puts the finishing touch on the whole operation. Array *r* now stores a bona fide (NULL-terminated) string.

The rest is quite simple. All we have to do is pass a pointer to *r* back to the calling program.

```
return(r);
```

This expression is the obvious and correct choice. Remember, *r* used without subscripting brackets is a pointer to the contents of this array. This address value is passed back to the calling program and assigned to pointer *p*. When *p* is handed to the cout stream, the display of "horsefly" is the result.

The complexities with this function lie in manually concatenating "fly" to "horse". The return of a pointer by the function is child's play. The following is an annotated listing of the function.

```
/* Return a char pointer to calling program */
char *combine(char *s, char *t)
{

        int x, y;/* x and y are ints */
        char r[100]; /* char array with 100 bytes */

        strcpy(r, s); /* copy s into r */
        y = strlen(r);/* return length of string */

        /* count x starting at y = x */
        for (x = y; *t != '\0'; ++x)
            r[x] = *t++; /*read byte from t into r*/

        r[x] = '\0';/* tack on NULL */

        return(r);/* return a pointer */

}
```

This program calls a function that *returns* a char pointer. It does not alter the object values of either of its two pointer arguments.

Summary

C++ functions may be viewed as completely separate programs. When called by any other entity, the function takes control. This control is not returned to the calling entity until the function returns a value (via the *return* statement) or until the function execution chain is completed.

Arguments are passed to functions *by value*. If *x* is an argument to a function, it is the value that *x* contains and not the variable and its assigned storage area that is passed. A like variable is created within the function to store the passed value in *x*.

We do not have access (within the function) to the variables themselves when they are used as arguments to functions. However, the address of a variable or other object in memory may be passed to a function, again, by value. When the function knows the address of an object in memory then it can directly address that object and make changes or retrieve information. If the value of an object is to be changed by a function, then the address of the object must be passed and not the value in the object.

When multiple arguments are passed to a function, an argument list is constructed in memory. Within the function, a pointer to the first argument can be used to access all of the list, provided that there is a specific indication of what kind and how many arguments were passed to the function. The inner workings of the printf() function access arguments in this manner, with the format string specifying the exact nature of the arguments that follow.

Pointers to functions are possible and practical. A function is not a variable, but it is possible to define pointers to functions that can be passed to other functions, placed in arrays, and used to manipulate data.

Functions are often used to read and write data in the calling program by being passed the memory address of an object. Likewise, it is quite simple to write a function that returns a memory address or pointer. To do this, the function must be prototyped in the calling program as a type that returns a pointer, as shown below.

```
char *combine();
```

In addition, the source code of the function must contain a heading of the return type.

```
char *combine(char *s, char *t)
```

These declarations inform the calling environment of the return *intentions* of the function.

The ability to incorporate new functions easily is a strong aspect of C++. Since these functions are actually separate programs that have no relationship with the calling program other than through the arguments that are specifically passed back and forth, pointers provide a direct means of communication. Passing memory addresses provide the function with a pathway into certain areas of the calling program. The function can then make changes and exchange information. Pointers are quite often the true power behind C++ function operations.

Chapter 8

Pointers and Structs

The pointers discussed so far have been of intrinsic data types and usually were directed to point to the address of a declared variable or to a known memory location to be read or written. A pointer can also be given the address of a function and can point to it. If you think about it long enough, you will soon realize that anything within a program lies in memory; therefore, a pointer can point to any part of the program, to any device driver, to any device interrupt.

The enhanced structs that are a part of C++ provide a means of defining a single variable that is actually comprised of a collection of many different data types. In more technical terms, we can say that a struct is a derived data type comprised of a collection of intrinsic data types. The specific collection of these intrinsic types actually forms the derived data type. In some ways, a struct can be compared to an array. The latter also provides a means of combining several variable storage areas into one accessed unit. In a struct, however, data do not have to be of the same type as is the case with an array.

The following code illustrates the most common form of a C++ struct.

```
struct dbase {
       char client[30];
       int acctnum;
       double amount;
};
```

This is a template for a struct named *dbase*, which is a collection of variables of different data types. The first struct element is a char array named *client*. The second and third are numeric types named *acctnum* and *amount*, respectively. This collection of variables may be accessed via the struct tag name, *dbase*. The following program shows one method of doing this.

```
struct dbase {
      char client[30];
      int acctnum;
      double amount;
};

#include <iostream.h>
#include <string.h>
int main()
{

      dbase r;

      strcpy(r.client, "Jones, M.");
      r.acctnum = 12;
      r.amount = 23917.33;

      cout << r.client << endl << r.acctnum << endl << r.amount <<
endl;

}
```

The following expression defines a variable named *r*, which is of type *dbase*.

```
dbase r;
```

Within the body of the program, the struct member operator (.) connects the struct name (*r*) and the member name. Therefore, *r.client* accesses the struct element *client[]* and is used as the target argument to strcpy(). The int and double members are assigned values using the same operator.

To display the contents of each struct element, the cout stream is invoked. Again the struct member operator comes into play with each of the arguments to this function.

Pointers to structs are very common in C++, so common that a special operator is used for accessing struct elements via pointers. The pointer to a struct member operator (->) is used to access a member of a struct using a pointer variable. The following program is a copy of the previous one, except that the struct elements are accessed via a pointer.

```
struct dbase {
     char client[30];
     int acctnum;
     double amount
};

#include <iostream.h>
#include <string.h>
int main()
{

     dbase r, *q;

     q = &r;

     strcpy(q->client, "Jones, M.");

     q->acctnum = 12;
     q->amount = 23917.33;

     cout << q->client << endl << q->acctnum << endl
<< q->amount << endl;


}
```

In this program example, the declaration below names *r* a variable of type *dbase* and *q* a pointer of the same type.

```
          dbase r, *q;
```

The next program line assigns *q* the address of *r*. Pointer *q* now points to the storage address reserved for struct *dbase*.

The pointer to a struct member operator is used to access each struct element. This special operator is simply a convenient shorthand method of access when dealing with pointers.

```
q->client
```

This expression means exactly the same thing as the one below.

```
(*q).client
```

In this latter example, the struct member operator and the indirection operator are used for access. The parentheses are necessary because the struct member operator takes higher precedence than does the indirection operator.

Pointers to structs are necessary when passing a whole struct to a function. C++ passes arguments to functions by value, so it is necessary to pass the address of the struct variable to the function to gain access to the data elements. The following program shows how this may be accomplished.

```
struct test {
      int a;
      char b;
      char name[20];
};
void load(struct test *);
#include <iostream.h>
#include <string.h>
int main()
{

      test r;

      load(&r);

      cout << r.a << " " << r.b << " " << r.name;

}
void load(struct test *s)
{

      s->a = 14;
```

```
        s->b = 'A';

        strcpy(s->name, "Group");

    }
```

A struct named *test* is defined with three elements of type int, char, and char array. Variable *r* is declared to be of type struct *test*. The load() function is called and is passed the memory address of *r* using the address-of operator. Within the function, *s* is declared a pointer of type struct *test*. This pointer has the address of the struct and uses the pointer to struct member operator to access each of the three struct members. Since *s* is a pointer, assignments are made to the memory locations of each of the elements. These values are written directly to the struct. Upon returning to the calling program, the values 14, A, and Group will be written on the screen.

When dealing with C++ structs, there is no problem with individual access of each element. However, when the struct as a whole is to be passed as an argument, a pointer to the struct is required. Pointers to structs have their own connective operators that allow for access in a convenient, shorthand manner. Trying to access a struct via a function call that does not include the struct address is an error and will result in garbage writes and reads within the struct.

Comparing Structs and Arrays

An array is an entity designed to store multiple quantities, all of which are of the same data type. For instance, a char array stores a continuous series of char data types. If the array is sized to contain 10 chars and the memory address of the beginning storage location is at 100, then the first element is stored at this location, the second is stored at 101, the third at 102, etc. The data are stored sequentially.

The same sequence applies to an array of ints, except that 2 bytes of storage are allocated for each element. Therefore, an int array whose initial storage address is 100 will store the first int value in bytes 100, 101. The second int value will be stored at 102, 103, the third at 104, 105, etc.

An array of floats with the same beginning address will store the first value in bytes 100, 101, 102, 103. The second quantity will be stored at 104, 105, 106, 107. The same 4-byte storage applies to long int types.

In every case, the storage units are aligned sequentially. An entire block of continuous memory is allocated for storage to any array, regardless of the type of data the array is to contain. The total memory allocated to the array depends on two factors: the data type and the value in the array subscript.

For char arrays, 10 chars may be stored in 10 bytes. For int arrays, 20 bytes will be required to store 10 values. With doubles, a total of 80 bytes will be required, as a double-precision floating-point value is stored in 8 bytes of memory. All of these quantities assume a standard MS-DOS implementation.

The key element here is that allocated storage for arrays is sequential, one continuous block of memory. We do not run into a situation where the first element in an array is stored at an address of 100, while the second is stored at an address of 1500. If the latter storage routine were used, accessing individual elements in an array would be very difficult, as the address of each element would have to be obtained by separate operations. Using C++, we know that if 10 elements were a part of a char array, each of these elements would be accessed as a sequential offset of the first element.

From a storage viewpoint, C++ structs are closely akin to arrays because all of the members are stored sequentially. Consider the following struct template.

```
struct employee {
    char dept;
    int tenure;
    double salary;

};
```

This derived type contains three intrinsic data types, a char, an int, and a double. If we assume that the address of the first array member (*dept*) is at location 100, then storage for int *tenure* begins at 101, offset 1 byte from the beginning storage location because 1 byte of storage is required for the char data type. Since an int consumes 2 bytes, storage for double *salary* begins at address 103, offset 2 bytes from the int member. Bytes 103 through 110 are allocated for double *salary* since a double value requires 8 bytes of storage.

Storage for a C++ struct is sequential, and it is closely akin to an array in this regard. The main distinction between the two is that different data types may be stored in a struct. We might think of a struct as an array of multiple quantities that may be of different data types.

The struct begins with a template, which is an appropriate name because the template is used to allocate memory. This allocation takes place by reading the number of members and their individual data types. The number of one data type is multiplied by the individual storage requirements for this data type to arrive at the necessary storage. When the storage values for the total number of each data type in the struct are added, the overall storage requirement for one instance of the struct is obtained.

When the program has this information, it can properly allocate memory for as many struct instances (variables) as are declared in the program. Struct *employee* requires 11 bytes of storage. Therefore, if a program declares four variables of type *employee*, a total of 44 bytes will be allocated in four discrete groups of 11 bytes each. We can say that such a program would have four instances of struct *employee*.

The following program details this allocation of structs.

```
struct e_record {
      char name[15];
      int id;
      int years;
      double sal;

};
#include <iostream.h>
#include <string.h>
int main()
{

      e_record emp;

      strcpy(emp.name, "Ken Jones");

      emp.id = 14;
      emp.years = 22;
      emp.sal = 535.00;

      cout << "Employee Name: " << emp.name << endl;
      cout << "Employee Number: " << emp.id << endl;
      cout << "Years Employed: " <<emp.years << endl;
      cout << "Employee Salary: $" << emp.sal;

}
```

When this program is executed, the following information will be displayed on the monitor.

```
Employee Name: Ken Jones
Employee Number: 14
Years Employed: 22
Employee Salary: $535.00
```

This program directly accesses struct members via the struct variable and the struct member operator. The struct pointer version of this program is shown below.

```
struct e_record {
      char name[15];
      int id;
      int years;
      double sal;

};
#include <iostream.h>
#include <string.h>
int main()
{

      e_record e, *emp;

      emp = &e;

      strcpy(emp->name, "Ken Jones");

      emp->id = 14;
      emp->years = 22;
      emp->sal = 535.00;

      cout << "Employee Name: " << emp->name << endl;
      cout << "Employee Number: " << emp->id << endl;
      cout << "Years Employed: " << emp->years <<
endl;
      cout << "Employee Salary: $" <<emp->sal;

}
```

In this source code, a struct variable is created along with a pointer of type struct *e_record*. Next, the pointer is given the address of the struct variable (*e*). The struct variable is necessary, because the compiler will allocate space for it upon declaration. Without the struct variable, the struct pointer has no size (is not initialized). A struct template simply tells the compiler how much space to allocate for the block of memory that will serve as storage for any struct variables. No automatic allocation occurs until a struct variable is declared.

As the following code demonstrates, we can write the previous program in a slightly different manner by using the *new* operator to allocate storage space, eliminating the need for a struct variable.

```
struct e_record {
      char name[15];
      int id;
      int years;
      double sal;

};
#include <iostream.h>
#include <string.h>
#include <stdlib.h>
int main()
{

      e_record *emp;

      emp = new e_record;
      if (emp == NULL)
            exit(0);

      strcpy(emp1->name, "Ken Jones");

      emp->id = 14;
      emp->years = 22;
      emp->sal = 535.00;

      cout << "Employee Name: " << emp->name << endl;
      cout << "Employee Number: " << emp->id << endl;
      cout << "Years  Employed:  "  <<  emp->years  <<
endl;
      cout << "Employee Salary: $" <<emp->sal;

}
```

This program will display the same screen data as did the previous two examples. Instead of creating a struct variable and then handing its address to the struct pointer, only the pointer is declared. The *new* operator is used to allocate the necessary space for the pointer. Note that the value in *emp* is tested for the occurrence of a NULL value. A NULL return would mean that memory could not be allocated, and the program would terminate when the exit() function was called.

Storage is automatically allocated when a struct variable is declared. However, if a struct pointer is declared, there is no automatic allocation for the struct members as is the case with any other type of declared pointer. The only memory allocated is 2 bytes for the struct pointer to store an address. Allocation for a struct pointer requires the use of the *new* operator or a memory allocation function such as malloc(). Without the use of *new* in the previous program, any assignments would have been made to an uninitialized pointer.

Even though the *new* operator determinesthe size of the data block needed, let's calculate the storage requirements for ourselves. Examine the struct template below.

```
struct e_record {
        char name[15];
        int id;
        int years;
        double sal;

}
```

From the earlier discussions in this chapter, you should now be able to determine the exact size of struct *e_record.* The calculations proceed as follows.

```
char name[15] = 15-bytes
int id=2-bytes
int years=2-bytes
double sal=8-bytes

Total Size= 27-bytes
```

The size of struct *e_record* is 27 bytes. The char array with 15 elements requires 15 bytes. Each int type requires 2 bytes, and the double type requires 8 bytes. Therefore, a variable of type *e_record* will be allocated 27 bytes of storage, the size of this derived data type.

We can verify this information by placing the following statement in the previous program.

```
cout << sizeof(struct e_record) << endl;
```

This will write a value of 27 to the monitor screen, the size that we have already calculated for struct *e_record* storage.

Let's compare this struct with an array. We know that the allocated storage for the struct is consecutive. Therefore, the first 15 bytes (of 27 total bytes) will be reserved for the char array member. The next 2 bytes are reserved for the first int member, while the 2 bytes that follow are reserved for the second int member. The last 8 bytes are allocated for the double member.

The following program will prove the contention that struct data are stored in one memory block of consecutive bytes.

```
struct e_record {
     char name[15];
     int id;
     int years;
     double sal;

};
#include <iostream.h>
#include <string.h>
int main()
{

     e_record emp;

     strcpy(emp.name, "Ken Jones");

     emp.id = 14;
     emp.years = 22;
     emp.sal = 535.00;

     cout << unsigned(&emp.name) << endl;
     cout << unsigned(&emp.id) << endl;
     cout << unsigned(&emp.years) << endl;
     cout << unsigned(&emp.sal) << endl;

}
```

On the system used for testing all applications in this book, the screen displayed the following.

```
65498
65513
65515
65517
```

Some simple math will show that the memory addresses are offset by the size of the data declared in the struct template. The first address in the listing above is the start of the *name* member. The next address is at a 15-byte offset from this address, the size of the char array. This second address is the location of the *id* data member, an int, so there is a 2-byte offset from this location to the next storage address for the *years* member, also an int. The last address is offset 2 bytes from the *years* location. We can safely assume that the end of the memory block allocated for the struct is located at address 65524, since 8 bytes are required for storage of a double value.

The program that shows the address location of each member in the struct has simply accessed the cout stream with pointers to each struct member accessed by the struct variable *emp*. Instead of returning the object value at each location, the address-of operator (&) causes each of the struct variable designations to return its address, which is cast to an unsigned int. This program proves that C++ structs store their data members in sequential blocks of memory.

The following program is a slight modification of an earlier one. It writes object values directly to the memory locations allocated for the struct. Following these assignments, the struct member object values are accessed by using the struct member operator.

```
struct e_record {
    char name[15];
    int id;
    int years;
    double sal;

};
#include <iostream.h>
#include <string.h>
int main()
{

    e_record emp;

    char *c;
    int *i, *h;
    double *d;

    c = &emp;/* Assign address in emp to c */

    i = c + 15; /* offset for id */
    h = c + 17; /* offset for years */

    d = c + 19; /* offset for sal */
```

```
/* Copy string into offset 0 of struct */
        strcpy(c, "Ken Jones");

/* Assign object values to offsets */
        *i = 14;
        *h = 22;
        *d = 535.00;

/* Extract struct data in normal manner */
        cout << "Employee Name: " << emp.name << endl;
        cout << "Employee Number: " << emp.id << endl;
        cout << "Years Employed: " << emp.years <<
endl;
        cout << "Employee Salary: $" << emp.sal <<
endl;

}
```

The monitor display will be identical to previous programs, but notice that the struct was never *loaded* with data in the traditional sense. Instead of accessing the allocated memory locations via the struct member operator (.) to make these assignments, these operations have taken place using pointers that were declared separately.

The address of the struct variable named *emp* is assigned to *c*, a pointer of type char. Next, the address of pointer *c* is used as the base reference for address assignments to two pointers of type int and one of type double. It is necessary to align the pointer types with the type of data they are to store. A char pointer was chosen for the base reference because of the offsets. Char pointers operate in units of 1 byte. If *c* had been declared an int pointer, then an offset value of *c + 15* would have resulted in an actual offset of 30 bytes from the base location because pointers are incremented in SSUs, not (necessarily) in bytes. With this in mind, incrementing a 2-byte int pointer by 15 SSUs would result in a 30-byte offset. The convenience of the 1-byte nature of char types is utilized here, although a void pointer could be made to serve as well, since it is also a 1-byte entity.

Once the proper offset addresses have been assigned, the referenced memory locations are assigned object values. Since, *i* and *h* are int pointers, the object values will be encoded into 2 bytes. The double pointer, *d*, will store its object value in an 8-byte encoded format. Copying the string to the char pointer is handled in a normal fashion using strcpy().

At this point in the program, the struct members have been fully assigned. Pointers have been used to *invade* the allocated memory set aside for the exclusive use of the struct variable. Even though separately declared pointers were used to access the memory locations allocated to the various struct members, the end result is exactly the same as if the assignments had been made using the conventional struct member operator in conjunction with the struct variable and the member names.

To prove this, the next portion of the program is identical to the earlier example from which it was derived. The cout stream arguments use struct member operators and struct member names. The result is the familiar display.

This roundabout method of dealing with structs is presented to alert the reader to some of the many internal intricacies that are carried out within the program whenever structs are accessed. You can be sure that internal pointer operations are in great abundance when structs are made a part of any C++ program. Since the process is transparent, most programmers don't fully appreciate all that goes on behind the scenes when structs are programmed. However, delving into the minuscule operations of almost any programming element that is a part of the C++ language will eventually reveal the hidden pointer operations that make the processes appear outwardly simple.

Summary

In C++, a struct is a collection of intrinsic data types that results in a single, derived data type. In many ways, a struct may be compared with an array, since storage is allocated for all struct members in one block of sequential memory. Storage for each member is based on its individual requirements. Member storage within the allocated block is arranged in the order in which such members are declared within the struct template.

Arrays are limited to storing data that are all of the same type. This limitation is not placed on a struct that stores a collection of different data types as a single unit.

Structs are such specialized tools that special operators have been developed to access their members. The struct member operator (.) directly accesses struct members, while the pointer to a struct member operator (->) accesses members via pointers.

Pointers to structs are absolutely essential when passing the struct to a function. Arguments to functions in C++ are passed by value, so the address of the struct must be handed to any function that is expected to affect operations on any of its members.

Chapter 9

Pointers and Unions

Many of the same principles of structs discussed in Chapter 8 apply equally to C++ unions. A union template is almost identical to a struct template save for the fact that the *union* keyword is used. Union members are declared in the same fashion. We even use the same operators for accessing union members.

Both a struct and a union allow for the combining of different data types in to create a derived type. However, a union does not have the capability of simultaneously storing more than one member object value, whereas a struct may store all member values at one time.

A union is a simple device that allows data of any type to be stored at a single memory location. When a union is created, an area of memory is allocated for storage. All union members reside at the same address. For this reason, any assignment to a union member automatically overwrites any previous assignment made to any other member of this same union.

Consider the following union template.

```
union alpha {
      int i;
      char a;
};
```

This union has two members, an int and a char. The total storage allocation for a union is handled differently than for a struct. With the latter, storage is based on the number of members of each data type multiplied by the storage requirement for each type. Storage allocation for a union is far simpler. Total union memory allocation is based on the minimum memory required to store its largest (from a storage viewpoint) data type.

In the example above, the union will be allocated a total storage quantity of 2 bytes, because the largest data member is an int, requiring 2 bytes in most MS-DOS C++ implementations. This quantity is adequate to store an int value and more than adequate to store a char value, the latter requiring only 1 byte.

```
union alpha {
      int i;
      char a;

};
#include <iostream.h>
int main()
{

      alpha r;

      r.i = 128;
      r.a = 'A';

      cout << r.i << endl;

}
```

This program will display a value of 65 on the monitor screen, not 128, because an assignment to any union member automatically overwrites any assignment made to any other member within the same union. In this example, the int member is assigned a value of 128. For the sake of discussion, let's assume that this value is stored in the 2 bytes beginning at address 100. Next, the char member is assigned a value of 'A'.

When the cout stream displays the value in the int member, this value has changed from the initial 128 to 65. The reason for this is that 'A' has an ASCII value of 65. This value overwrites the single byte at address 100 that was originally used to store 128. Byte 101 stored a 0, 128 and 0 being the 2-byte (int) code for 128. When the cout stream accesses bytes 100 and 101, the 2-byte encoding is now 65 and 0, the int code for a value of 65 decimal. This proves that a C++ union is allocated only one memory block for all union members and that only one member may contain a useful value at any time.

In simplest terms, a union contains a set of members that share the same memory address. The union members are accessed via the struct/union member operator (.) or a struct/union pointer to a member operator (->).

The following program example performs some simple operations using a union.

```
union test {
        int x;
        float y;
        double z;
};

int main()
{

        test a;

        a.x = 19;
        a.y = 131.334;
        a.z = 9.9879;


}
```

Nothing is displayed on the monitor when this program is executed because it just assigns variables.

We might think of a union as a generic pointer to a specific memory location that may be used to store all types of data at this single address. In this program, variables *a.x*, *a.y*, and *a.z* share the same memory address.Each union member assignment overwrites the one made previously. The last union member assignment is the only one that remains in memory. The storage space allocated to this union is 8 bytes, as this is the size needed to store the largest union member (double).

The C++ union is may be thought of as a specialized pointer. To illustrate this concept, the program above can be completely rewritten using pointers, as follows.

```
#include <stdlib.h>
int main()
{

    int *x;
    float *y;
    double *z;

    z = new double;
    if ((z == NULL)
        exit(0);

    y = (float *) z;
    x = (int *) z;

    // x, y, and z all contain the same address
    // memory allocation is for a double type

    *x = 19;
    *y = 131.334;
    *z = 9.9879;



}
```

Three pointers of type int, float, and double are declared. The *new* operator is used to allocate enough memory for a double data type. Next, each of the pointers is handed the address in z. At this juncture, they all point to the same memory location, an area that has been allocated enough storage to contain a double-precision floating-point value. Like a union, the variables all share the same address and memory has been allocated for the largest variable type. Also like a union, each time an object value is assigned, it overwrites the previous object value of any other variable. In a union, only one member can be *active* at a time, and this condition has been set up in the last program by using pointers.

This works as well as the union example but only from an execution standpoint. For such applications, a union is far more efficient than using pointers, as all of the storage and addressing is handled by the union declaration. The access allowed by the union avoids the use of convoluted pointer operations like those shown above.

The following program declares a union pointer and accesses data members using the pointer operator.

```
union test {
int x;

        float y;
        double z;
};
#include <iostream.h>
#include <stdlib.h>
int main()
{

        test *ptr;

        ptr = new test;
        if (ptr == NULL)
              exit(0);

        cout << sizeof(test) << endl;

        ptr->x = 19;
        ptr->y = 131.334;
        ptr->z = 9.9879;


}
```

This program will display a value of 8 on the monitor because the size of the storage allocated to this union is 8 bytes. As we already know, the maximum size of any union is the same as the size of its largest data member, in this case, a double-precision floating-point type.

Unions and Memory Conservation

The simple program examples used for tutorial purposes in this book do not place a strain on memory, at least in normal execution environments. Certainly, a premium can be placed on memory conservation when program code begins to take on gigantic proportions. However, what is meant by *gigantic* proportions?

This is a relative term that is best referenced against the amount of memory available within a system. Some commercial programs go to great and expensive lengths to conserve memory use during execution. One factor is the desire to stay within the 640K base memory limit to avoid the use of extended or expanded memory. When these other areas of memory must be utilized, one must consider the limits of the machines that typical buyers use. Currently, a 2-megabyte limit is placed on many types of high-level general applications software. This means that all programs written for this class of buyer should require no more than 2 megabytes of RAM to be fully operational. Other buyer classes may apply different limits. For example, high-level CAD (computer-aided design) programs typically require a minimum of 4 megabytes of RAM, with 8 and even 16 megabytes required for many of the latest offerings in this area.

There is another factor that relegates even the smaller programs into the gigantic category. These are called *TSRs* (terminate-and-stay-resident) and *ISRs* (interrupt service routine). Such programs remain in memory at all times, consuming RAM while other programs are executed in the foreground. When triggered (often by the touch of a single or multiple key combination), these memory-resident programs become active.

Since programs of this type constantly consume a portion of RAM, it is essential that they be made as small as possible. This is a situation where every byte of savings is precious. Given such a set of circumstances, the C++ union becomes a very valuable programming tool.

A union is allocated one block of memory, sized to the requirements of its largest single data member. The largest single intrinsic data type is a double. However, unions and structs may also contain arrays of any type as data members. Here, size can grow to monstrous proportions. Structs can also be members of other structs or of unions. Union members may even consist of other unions. The capability of combining many different data types, intrinsic and derived, allows both structs and unions to form very complex and large derived data types.

The following program does not use a union but depends upon two structs to amass data types.

```
struct e_record {
char name[15];
     int id;
     int years;
     double sal;
};

struct a_record {

     char name[15];
     char address[40];
};

#include <iostream.h>
```

```
#include <string.h>
int main()
{

        e_record v;
        a_record w;

        strcpy(v.name, "Bill Collins");
        v.id = 44;
        v.years = 12;
        v.sal = 351.22;

        cout << "Name: " << v.name << endl;
        cout << "Identification: << v.id << endl;
        cout << "Tenure: << v.years << endl;
        cout << "Salary: $" << v.sal << endl;

        strcpy(w.address, "523 Short St.; Front Royal,
VA22630");
        strcpy(w.name, "Bill Collins");

        cout << "Name: " w.name << endl;
        cout << "Address: "<<% w.address << endl;



}
```

The *e_record* struct is identical to one used in Chapter 8, but the *a_record* struct has been added, and it contains two data members, a char array sized to 15 bytes to store a name and another char array of 40 characters to store an address. This is a tutorial example that has been made as simple as possible. The *a_record* struct might just as easily have included twenty or more data members.

In this usage, the structs are incorporated to help in grouping the data needed for some type of employee record. We will assume that the employee's address is kept separate from the other data for some reason such as creating a mailing list.

When this program is executed, it will display the following on the monitor.

```
Name: Bill Collins
Identification:44
Tenure: 12 years
Salary: $351.22

Name: Bill Collins
Address: 523 Short St.; Front Royal, VA22630
```

This program utilizes two structs and declares a variable for each struct type. How much storage has been allocated for the structs?

We already know from Chapter 8 that struct *e_record* will be allocated 27 bytes. Calculating storage for struct *a_record* is simple, as we simply add the two subscript values in the array declarations, arriving at an allocation figure of 55 bytes. Total storage for both structs is 82 bytes.

Notice that the second struct is utilized only after the first struct has been loaded and handed to the cout stream. At this point in the program, struct *e_record* is no longer needed. However, it has been created, and its memory allocation will remain in effect until the program is terminated.

Now, let's bring a union into the picture and try to improve on memory consumption.

```
struct e_record {
     char name[15];
     int id;
     int years;
     double sal;
};

struct a_record {
     char name[15];
     char address[40];
};

union com {
     e_record a;
     a_record b;
};

#include <iostream.h>
#include <string.h>
int main()
{

     union com v;

     strcpy(v.a.name, "Bill Collins");

     v.a.id = 44;
     v.a.years = 12;
     v.a.sal = 351.22;
```

```
         cout << "Name: " << v.name << endl;
         cout << "Identification: << v.id << endl;
         cout << "Tenure: << v.years << endl;
         cout << "Salary: $" << v.sal << endl;

         strcpy(v.b.name, "Bill Collins");
         strcpy(v.b.address, "523 Short St.; Front Royal, VA22630");
         cout << "Name: " << v.b.name << endl;
         cout << "Address: " << v.b.address << endl;



   }
```

The display from this program is exactly like the one that preceded it. However, what is our memory consumption now that the union has been made a part of this latest example? Examine the union template below.

```
         union com {
               struct e_record a;
               struct a_record b;
         }
```

This union contains two data members, each a struct. We know that *e_record* is allocated 27 bytes of storage and that *a_record* is allocated 55 bytes. However, this is a union, so storage is allocated for only the largest data member. Therefore, the total storage allocation is 55 bytes, not 82 bytes as was the case when two structs were utilized without the union. There has been a savings of 27 bytes because only a single union variable is declared. This represents an approximate 33 percent decrease in storage for the struct elements in comparison with the earlier program, a sizable percentage factor. However, it won't be appreciated in a simple program of this size. When data groupings grow to 100K or more bytes, this process becomes far more valuable.

Unions allow one area of memory to be used for the storage of many different program data elements. Obviously, multiple use of the same memory location is going to result in a savings when compared with storing all data elements in their own exclusive memory areas.

If we were to include the following line in this program, the size of the union would also be displayed during the execution run.

```
         cout << sizeof(com) << endl;
```

The display value would be 55, the storage requirement of the largest struct in union *a_record*.

Summary

Unions operate in a manner that is comparable to a special pointer that may be used to reference a memory location to store any type of data. While a struct template and a union template are declared in much the same manner, there are vast differences in how each of these stores data.

A union is allocated a memory block that is adequate to store its largest data member. An assignment to any member automatically overwrites any previous assignment to any other union member. This occurs because all assignments to union members are stored at the same location.

Unions may be incorporated for many purposes, especially where it is necessary to control the size of memory allocation. The manipulation of such data must lend itself to the limited duration of data existence since every assignment made to a union member is overwritten by any other assignment that may follow.

Due to the specialized nature of a union and its parallel operation with C++ structs, the two entities share the same access operators. What was described earlier as the struct member operator (.) becomes the union member operator when used to access unions. The same applies to the struct/union pointer operator.

Chapter 10

Pointers and C++ Classes

Object-oriented programming (OOP) via C++ involves classes. A C++ class is the true object in object-oriented programming. It is a user-defined type. In ANSI C a new data type is subject to the rules of usage of standard (intrinsic) data types. This is not entirely true in C++, where the programmer is allowed to define not only the contents of a class but also the behavior of that class.

A class object should be thought of as a unique entity, unlike any other data type. The class is the object in OOP, and rules of behavior of such an object are determined by the programmer who writes these rules into the class object. An object actually causes itself to be created and destroyed. The exact nature of its creation is part of the class personality. The class also determines how it may and may not be manipulated. Access to the components of the class object is governed by the rules that are defined and contained within the class. Generally, a class may not be accessed by the built-in operators and functions contained in the C++ language unless it specifically allows for such access.

The class object may even be thought of as a mini-world. It contains its own rules of natural order, access, manipulation, and interaction. It may even pass on some or all of these properties to another class object that is said to inherit from the original, or *base*, class.

Classes and Structs

While there are many operational similarities between C++ enhanced structs and C++ classes, they are entirely different in concept. Such differences may seem subtle, but classes are traditionally used for an OOP approach while C++ structs are used for procedural-based operations. This convention is strictly adhered to by most programmers; however, any structs within a C++ program may be renamed classes and the execution characteristics will not change. In fact, a C++ struct is implemented as a class within the internal framework of the compiler. Again, using classes for OOP and structs for procedural-based applications is a convention that clearly separates the two types of programming methods and the tools that are used for each.

The similarity between the class and the struct is carried over into the operators used for access. When dealing with classes, what is commonly known as the struct member operator (.) becomes the class member operator. A pointer to a class member uses the familiar (->) operator.

C++ classes may contain not only data members but also member functions. When functions are declared or defined within the class, they are more properly called *methods*. C++ structs may also contain member functions, but this type of use is not often seen, since it is more appropriate to commit such operations to classes. Again, a class and a struct can operate in exactly the same manner within the C++ environment, but it is customary to use structs for procedural-based programming and classes for OOP.

The program example that follows uses a class that contains data members and methods (member functions).

```
#include <iostream.h>
#include <string.h>
class person {
    private:
        int age;
        char name[50];
    public:
        void assign(int x, char *c);
        void display(void);
};
int main()
{
```

```
            person male, female;
            male.assign(32, "Robert F. Franklin");
            female.assign(27, "Grace E. Miller");
            male.display();
            female.display();
      }
    void person::assign(int i, char *s) {
          age = i;
          strcpy(name, s);
    }
    void person::display(void)
    {

            cout << name << " is " << age << " years old." <<
      endl;

      }
```

When executed, the program will display the following information on the monitor screen.

```
            Robert F. Franklin is 32 years old.
            Grace E. Miller is 27 years old.
```

This program creates two objects, *male* and *female*. These are objects of class *person*. Notice that the member of class operator (.) is used to access each of the class methods as in

```
            male.display()
```

This invokes the display() method of the *male* object that is of type *person*. This is direct access of the class method, but it is quite easy to accomplish the same operations via pointers to a class. The following program comprises a slight rewrite of the previous example to show how pointers to classes are manipulated.

```
      #include <iostream.h>
      #include <string.h>
      class person {
            private:
                  int age;
                  char name[50];
```

```
            public:
                  void assign(int x, char *c);
                  void display(void);
};
int main()
{

        person *male, *female;

        male = new person;
        female = new person;

        male->assign(32, "Robert F. Franklin");
        female->assign(27, "Grace E. Miller");

        male->display();
        female->display();

}
void person::assign(int i, char *s) {

        age = i;
        strcpy(name, s);

}
void person::display(void)
{

        cout << name << " is " << age << " years old." <<
endl;

}
```

In this example, *male* and *female* are declared pointers of type *person*. Since a pointer has only enough storage to contain an address value, it is necessary to allocate additional storage for the entire class content. This is accomplished using the *new* operator. The following assignments cause the pointers of type *person* to point to allocated areas of memory that are sized to match exactly the storage needs of *person* class objects.

```
        male = new person;
        female = new person;
```

The *person* designation following the *new* operator is a data type just as int, double, char, etc. are data types. The latter are intrinsic types, while *person* is a user-defined type. The *new* operator uses the *person* designation as a size determinant. Therefore, a memory block is allocated that is the exact size needed for storage of an object of class *person*. Within the program portion under main(), the pointer to a class member operator (->) is used to access the members of the class object.

Class Member Alignment

In C++, class data members are aligned in the same manner as struct data members. Data are lumped into a single sequential memory block. However, this applies only to the data members. Each time a class object is declared, all data members in the class template are replicated. However, class methods are created only once. This single set of member functions is referenced by each class object that is created. Again, class methods are not duplicated each time a new class object is declared.

The following program uses the person class to illustrate the alignment of class data objects.

```
#include <iostream.h>
#include <string.h>

    class person {
        private:
            int age;
            char name[50];
        public:
            void assign(int x, char *c);
            void display(void);

};

int main()
{

    person male;
    int *c;

    c = (int *) &male;

    male.assign(45, "Frank Smith");
```

```
        cout << *c << endl;

        cout << (char *) ++c << endl;

}
void person::assign(int i, char *s) {

        age = i;
        strcpy(name, s);

}
void person::display(void)
{

        cout << name << " is " << age << " years old." <<
endl;

}
```

This program will display

```
    45
    Frank Smith
```

on the monitor. Notice that this has been done by tapping directly into the memory area reserved for data member storage of the *male* object.

The *male* object is declared a variable of type *person*. Next, a standard int pointer is declared and assigned the address in the *male* object by using the address-of operator preceding the variable name. At this juncture, the int pointer has the address of the *male* object.

If we assume that the class data members are stored sequentially, then *c* should return the value of 45 that has been assigned to the first data member, and ++*c* should access the string copied into the *name* array within the class.

Using the cout stream, the storage arrangement and alignment are revealed. Indeed, the base address of the object is the storage location of the first data member. Since this member is an int type, it must be allotted 2 bytes of storage. This is the reason that an int pointer was used for access, although a char pointer would have served as well, providing that the proper increments were effected before the next data element (*name*) was accessed.

The display of information contained within the data members was managed without resorting to the display() member function because the exact nature of the class template was known. This program has simply read information from the loaded data elements and displayed it on the screen. Another way of revealing the data member alignment within this class involves direct writes to the members, as shown in the following program.

```cpp
#include <iostream.h>
#include <string.h>

class person {
        private:
                int age;
                char name[50];
        public:
                void assign(int x, char *c);
                void display(void);

};
int main()
{

        person male;
        int *c;

        c = (int *) &male;
        *c++ = 45;
        strcpy((char *) c, "Frank Smith");

        male.display();

}
void person::assign(int i, char *s) {

        age = i;
        strcpy(name, s);

}
void person::display(void)
{

        cout << name << " is " << age << " years old." <<
endl;

}
```

This program will display

```
Frank Smith is 45 years old.
```

The monitor write was handled by the display() method, but notice that the assign() method was never called. The assignment of data members was made by direct access to the class object memory storage area. This operation is a reverse of the one in the previous example where the memory area contents were read directly.

Again, this example bears out the fact that class data members are stored sequentially in a starting memory location that serves as the base address of the class object. Data members are stored in the order in which they are declared in the class template. In these examples, the *age* variable was declared before the *name* array, so the storage area for *age* precedes that of *name*. In these examples, we can safely say that if *male* is a class object, then &*male* points to the storage area for the first data member of the *male* object.

Be advised that directly accessing class members by tapping into their exclusive storage areas is not a standard procedure by any means and is not recommended for general programming applications. The operations carried out in these examples are meant to further reveal the data alignment within classes. While there are alternative means of accessing the contents of a class and circumventing the safety features provided by *private* and *protected* access, these are of no use to a programmer other than as a tutorial exercise.

Virtual Functions and Member Alignment

Previous examples in this chapter have involved classes that contained data elements and standard member functions (methods). However, C++ has introduced the *virtual function* as well. This is a special function that is defined in a base class and then may be redefined in any derived class.

When virtual functions are made a part of a C++ class, the rules of alignment change slightly. To clearly illustrate this point, consider the following simplified program example that includes a class comprised of a single data element and a two (non-virtual) functions.

```
#include <iostream.h>
class alpha {
    private:
          int x;
    public:
          void assign(int y)
          {

                x = y;

          }
```

```
                         void display()
                         {
                                  cout << x << endl;
                         }
        };
        int main()
        {

                alpha test;
                int *i = (int *) &test;

                test.assign(4);
                test.display();

                cout << "x resides at " << unsigned(i) << endl;
                cout << "The value in i is " << *i << endl;

        }
```

This program uses two standard member functions and a single int variable to comprise the *alpha* class. Our experiences in previous program examples in this chapter tell us that exclusive storage for variable *x* will be located at *&test*, the class object. This is proven to be correct when the program is executed.

```
        4
        x resides at 65524
        The value in i is 4
```

The 65524 value may be different depending on exact machine and software configurations.

This example tells us that the exclusive storage area for the class variable is at 65524 in the 64K data segment. This is further verified by displaying the value at this location, which is identical to the value produced by the display() method.

There is nothing unusual about this exercise; it duplicates the results of the previous examples in this chapter. However, change the class methods to virtual types and all the rules will seem to change. The following code modifies the methods to virtual types while making no additional changes.

```
        #include <iostream.h>
```

```
class alpha {
      private:
            int x;
      public:
            virtual void assign(int y)
            {

                  x = y;

            }
            virtual void display()
            {

                  cout << x << endl;

            }

};
int main()
{
      alpha test;
      int *i = (int *) &test;

      test.assign(4);
      test.display();

      cout << "x resides at " << unsigned(i) << endl;
      cout << "The value in i is " << *i << endl;
}
```

When this modified program was executed on the test system, the display read as follows.

```
4
x resides at 65522
The value in i is 203
```

The values of 65522 and 203 may differ on the reader's system, but the point is that 65522 cannot be the storage location for class data member *x* or the object value at this location would match the value produced by the display() member function. Therefore, it must be assumed that the value in pointer *i* is not the offset for the class object as was the case in previous examples. The reason for the change in data alignment must be tied to declaring the member functions virtual types, since the virtual declaration was the only change made to the program example prior to this one. What are we dealing with here?

A bit of research is in order. If pointer *i*, which contains the address of *test*, is not the address of the single class data item, perhaps *i + 1* contains this object value. Change the contents under main() from the previous program to those that follow to find out.

```
int main()
{

        alpha test;
        int *i = (int *) &test;

        test.assign(4);
        test.display();

        cout << "x resides at " << unsigned(i + 1) << endl;
        cout << "The value in i + 1 is " << *(i + 1) << endl;
}
```

When this program was executed, it produced the following display using the test system.

```
4
x resides at 65524
The value in i is 4
```

This is exactly what was displayed on the test system prior to declaring the class methods virtual. However, the offset into the pointer address is no longer 0 but 1. That is, the pointer address incremented by one SSU unit now contains the base address for the data member in this class.

This is a bit of a mystery. We know that declaring the class methods virtual caused a different alignment within the class object. The data member is no longer located at the base address for the class object. It is removed by one SSU. The object value at the class base address is 203 (using the test system). What does this value mean? What is it used for? The answer to these questions must somehow be linked to the use of the virtual methods within the class.

Let's look again at virtual functions in general, especially when comparing them to standard, non-virtual functions. The latter reside as single entities in memory. The address of a function is returned in normal C++ syntax by using the function name without the parens. When a non-virtual function is made a part of a class, the function is called by using the class object name connected to the class member operator and the actual function name. In the case of a pointer to a class object, the pointer to a class member operator is used.

Making a virtual function a member of a class automatically causes the compiler to rearrange the storage order of the class. Storage is still sequential, but the first value (at offset 0 into the allocated memory for the class object) is a pointer to a table of virtual function pointers. These latter pointer values are the address locations of the virtual functions.

This means that the value of 203 from the previous example is the location of the table that contains a list of pointers to the virtual functions. The following program explores this table further.

```
#include <iostream.h>
class alpha {
      private:
             int x;
      public:
             virtual void assign(int y)
             {

                    x = y;

             }
             virtual void display()
             {

                    cout << x << endl;

             }
};
int main()
{

      alpha test;
      int *h, *i = (int *) &test;

      h = (int *) *i;

      cout << "1st method address = " << hex << *h++ <<
endl;
      cout << "2nd method address = " <<hex << *h << endl;

}
```

An additional int pointer (*h*) is declared in this program. It is assigned the object value in the *i* pointer. This is equal to 203 as in the previous example. This is the offset into the 64K segment where the virtual function look-up table is located. Using the cout stream, the two object values stored at this beginning location (203) are displayed on the monitor.

The test system configuration with Borland C++ Version 3.1 displayed the following text lines.

```
1st method address = 378
2nd method address = 388
```

These are hexadecimal values for the offset addresses of the two methods. The reason for using hex values here is to match the numbers base the Borland Turbo Debugger uses when it displays addresses of program variables. As soon as the previous program displayed the contents of the function table at offset 203 (decimal) into the 64K segment, Borland Turbo Debugger was executed. Selecting Variables under the View menu item, the address of each variable and function in the program is charted.

The result of the Turbo Debugger run on this program was to show that the assign() method's address is at absolute memory location 80F1:0378 and that display() is found at 80F1:0388. Here, 80F1 is the absolute location of the 64K segment that contains the data for the program. The offset into this segment is 378 and 388 hex, respectively. These values match the contents from the look-up table, so the mystery of just what is found at the base address of a class object containing virtual member functions has been completely solved.

Armed with this information, the data alignment within a class can be described as follows. If we assume that *p* is a pointer to a class object, then *p* is also a pointer to the first data member contained in the class object if non-virtual methods are used. If the class contains virtual methods, then *p* is a pointer to a table of addresses of these methods, and ++*p* is a pointer to the first data member in the class.

In fact, both of these alignments are quite similar. All data are contained in a single sequential block. However, when virtual methods are incorporated into a class, the table of pointers is the first data member followed by the declared data members within the class. Even though the table of pointers to the virtual methods is not specifically written by the programmer, it is still a data member that is necessary to the proper operation of the class object. The compiler actually writes this table into existence, based on the storage locations of the virtual methods at run time.

Since C++ enhanced structs are implemented as a type of class, the same alignment order applies to these when incorporating member functions and virtual member functions. However, structs are traditionally used to implement procedural-based programming, while classes are the true objects in OOP.

Summary

The alignment of data members within classes does not differ greatly from the alignment of data in C++ structs and arrays. In each case, there is a single storage block with data aligning in the order in which it is declared. The single exception to this occurs when classes utilize virtual methods. When this is done, the compiler generates a look-up table of pointers that identifies the location of each virtual function. The address of this table is the first data member (invisible) in the class followed by the declared data members within the class template.

Pointers to class objects are quite common and may be used to access class data and methods using the pointer to a class member operator (->). This is the same operator symbol used for accessing struct and union members via pointers.

Declaring pointers of intrinsic types (int, char, long, etc.) and using them to access class data can be easily accomplished, but this is not a type-safe way of programming. Examples of this procedure in this chapter have been used only to dissect class members for tutorial purposes. This form breaks every rule of object-oriented programming and is not recommended for general programming applications.

Chapter 11

Pointers to Pointers

The majority of discussions involving pointers in this book has dealt with the ability of these variables to store addresses. However, pointers have addresses, too. This is not the address assigned as a pointer object but the exclusive address of each pointer that is declared.

Small-memory model C++ compilers default to 2-byte pointers, while large models use 4-byte types. This refers to the exclusive area set aside for each declared pointer to store an address object assigned to it. We know that all standard variables have two values. The first is an address value, the place in memory where data are stored. The second is an object value, the data that are stored at the exclusive address.

What makes pointers a little more difficult to understand is that their object values are memory addresses. However, like all variables, pointers have two values as well. The first is the address value where storage is set aside for the pointer to store its object. The second value is the object value, but in this case, the object is another address.

Thus, pointers must have fixed addresses in which to store their objects. After all, storage cannot be accomplished without allocated memory. These fixed addresses, like the fixed addresses of other variable types, cannot be changed by the programmer. The following program illustrates this point.

```
#include <iostream.h>
int main()
{

    int *x;
    char *a;
    long *y;
    double *d;

    cout << unsigned(&x) << endl;
    cout << unsigned(&a) << endl;
    cout << unsigned(&y) << endl;
    cout << unsigned(&d) << endl;


}
```

Here's our old friend, the address-of operator (&), that is used in front of variable names to return their address values. In this example, the same operator is used in front of pointer names to return their address values. Therefore, if *x* is a declared pointer, then the following expression is a pointer to a pointer.

```
&x
```

This expression returns the memory address that pointer *x* uses to store its object value, which is another memory address. In most programming assignments, it is seldom necessary to access the exclusive storage address used by pointers, but the following program shows what is possible. This example exercises the pointer-to-a-pointer concept in a rather roundabout way.

```
#include <iostream.h>
#include <string.h>
int main()
{

    char *b, c[10];
    int x, *a;

    strcpy(c, "Goodbye");

    b = "HELLO";
    a = &b;
    x = &c[0];
```

```
        *a = x;

        cout << b << endl;
}
```

During execution, what will this program display on the screen when *b* is handed to the cout stream? Variable *b* is a char pointer that is initially assigned the address of the constant "HELLO". The correct answer is the following string.

```
Goodbye
```

This is displayed when the object at the address in *b* is written to the screen. How can this be?

First of all, we must look at strcpy() that copies "Goodbye" into *c*, a char array. Next, *b* is assigned the address of "HELLO", the constant value that you probably thought would be displayed by this program. However, the plot thickens!

Pointer *a* is now assigned the address of pointer *b*, using the address-of operator to gain access to the exclusive storage area of the latter pointer. The expression *&b* is a pointer to a pointer. Now, *x*, an auto variable of type int, is assigned the address of the char array. No, *x* is not a pointer, but there is no law that says it can't be assigned a memory address, as long as that address is in the normal integer range.

In this usage, *x* doesn't point to *c*, as a standard variable can't *point*. The value stored in *x* also happens to be the same value as an address location, but this is not a pointer to that address. In other words, array *c* cannot be directly accessed via *x*, but access can be gained indirectly.

The finishing touch involves writing the address value that is contained in *x* to the memory location pointed to by *a*. Remember, *a* has the address of the exclusive storage area for pointer *b*. This area has been invaded, violated, and changed to a new address, that of array *c* that points to the bytes containing "Goodbye". Notice that *a* was declared a pointer of type int. This means that **a = x* writes the value in *x* as a 2-byte integer to the address pointed to by *a*. Two bytes are assigned to pointers using the small-memory model compiler option, so an int pointer is the logical type to use for changing the object address in any pointer.

All of these assignments form a tail-chasing regimen that results in simply assigning *b* the address location of *c*. The easy way to effect this operation would be to replace all of the code following

```
        b = "HELLO";
```

with

```
        b = c;
```

That's all the varied assignments and hidden manipulations did in the program above.

In fact, the ridiculous avenues traveled in this latest example are on a par with the contents of a char array being changed by a function that has been passed the address of the array. The only difference here is that the memory address object in *b* was being altered by a pointer that had *b*'s memory address. To aid you further in understanding the previous program, it is presented again with comments.

```
#include <iostream.h>
#include <string.h>
int main()
{

    char *b, c[40];
    int x, *a;

    strcpy(c, "Goodbye"); /* Copy constant into c */

    b = "HELLO"; /* assign b memory address of HELLO */

    a = &b;/* read STORAGE address of b into a */
        /* Note: a is an int pointer; b is a char pointer */

    x = &c[0];/* Variable x is assigned address VALUE */
        /* x is not a pointer. Its object value */
        /* is an integer that equals the address */
        /* of &c[0]. */

    *a = x; /* Write value in x as an int (2-bytes) to *a */
        /* *a accesses two bytes of memory as its storage unit */

    cout << b << endl;/* Display what b points to */

}
```

Declared Pointers to Pointers

The concept of a pointer having the exclusive storage address of another pointer is, perhaps, a bit exotic but not highly unusual in C++. In most applications, you don't see pointers to pointers very often, but they can and do exist.

The previous program was a beginning exercise in working with pointers to pointers within the framework of what we have already discussed. However, a pointer to a pointer is a valid variable in C++ and is specially declared. The following program demonstrates this.

```
#include <iostream.h>
int main()
{

    int x, *p, **ptp;

    x = 1628;
    p = &x;
    ptp = &p;

    cout << unsigned(p) << endl;
    cout << **ptp << endl;

}
```

In this program **ptp* is declared a pointer to a pointer of type int. This means that *ptp* expects to be handed the address of a pointer. Variable *x* is assigned a value of 1628, then its address is assigned to pointer *p*. Next, the address of pointer *p* is assigned to pointer to a pointer *ptp*. The cout stream is written to better illustrate the results. Think of the pointer to a pointer in the following manner.

```
*(*ptp)
```

This may make the concept a little easier to comprehend. This program will display the memory address of pointer *p* and then the object value of 1628. When dealing with pointers to pointers, we must keep track of the indirection operators (*). The following expression accesses the object of the pointer whose address is held by the pointer to a pointer.

```
**ptp
```

However, the expression below returns the address assigned to the pointer to a pointer.

```
*ptp
```

We can even make the situation more bizarre. Assuming that ptp is a pointer to a pointer, the expression below is a *pointer to a pointer to a pointer.*

```
&ptp
```

The following program demonstrates the use of a pointer to a pointer of type char.

```
#include <iostream.h>
#include <string.h>
int main()
{

    char a[20], *b, **c;

    strcpy(a, "President");

    b = a;
    c = &b;

    cout << *c << " " << **c << endl;
}
```

This program will display the following string.

```
President P
```

Remember, a pointer to a pointer is a pointer within a pointer as well. The indirection operator is used to differentiate the objects being sought. If we think of *c* in this program as **(*c)*, then **c* returns the address handed to *c* in the following assignment line.

```
c = &b;
```

**c accesses the ultimate object that the *pointer that is pointed to points to.* That's quite a mouthful, but we are faced with a system of stacked pointers. Most programmers refer to these as nested pointers, but thinking of them as stacked is usually clearer. It is the *object* that is nested and not the pointers. At the bottom of the heap in a pointer stack is the ultimate object. Above that object is a pointer that points to it. Above that pointer is a pointer to a pointer. To get to the object, you have to start at the top with the pointer to a pointer, go through the pointer, and finally access the object.

In the program above, **c* is the memory address of the nested object, passed to the pointer to a pointer by the pointer whose address it was assigned. The expression **c* is the object at the bottom of the stack. In order to display a string, the string address is passed to the cout stream. This is what *c* is in the above program, while **c* is the 1-byte object at the same address that returns the first character in the string.

In C++, we can create as high a stack of pointers as we wish. The following program reaches utterly ridiculous proportions.

```
#include <iostream.h>
int main()
{

        int x, *p, **ptp, ***ptptp, ****ptptptp;

        x = 238;
        p = &x;
        ptp = &p;
        ptptp = &ptp;
        ptptptp = &ptptp;

        cout << ****ptptptp << endl;

}
```

As you might have guessed, this program displays the object value of 238 on the screen.

Understand that this is not a practical program. The chances of encountering such a monstrosity in a working program are very slim. However, this example does demonstrate the *deeply nested* capabilities of pointer operations, and it is important to understand the principle of pointers to pointers should an application arise where you can make use of this programming tool.

Summary

Like all variables, pointers have two values. The one most discussed is the rvalue or object value. However, a pointer's object value is an address. We normally think of the lvalue as being an address. A pointer also has an lvalue, which is the address location of storage assigned exclusively to the pointer. This is where it stores its object that is the address of (presumably) another object.

When a pointer is declared to receive the lvalue or address of another pointer, then it is known as a pointer to a pointer. We can stack these pointers many layers high, although most applications do not take the nesting to the extent some examples did in this chapter.

While you will not see a pressing need to resort to pointers to pointers, it is important to understand the concept, so that you may use this feature of C++ when best programming efficiency and expression demand such operations.

Chapter12

Source Code Format

This final chapter deals solely with common sense information that can make a major difference in understanding C++ and its many exotic, interesting, and powerful features. Understanding any language begins with the examination of source code. How this source code is presented seems to be taken for granted by a large number of C++ programmers, which can make learning the language difficult.

Source code should always be written in a simple, easy-to-read format. The following program is an example.

```
#include <iostream.h>
#include <string.h>

int main()
{

    int x;
    char a[40];

    strcpy(a, "Format");

    for (x = 0; x <= 10; ++x)
        cout << a << endl;


}
```

This program is very expressive and easy to comprehend because it is written in a style that expresses its intent. The main() function falls on the left hand margin. The opening brace is on this same margin immediately below the function name. Then, there is a blank line, a separation.

Next, the declaration block appears, indented five spaces. All declarations are made in this block that is then differentiated by another blank line. While C++ allows variables to be declared at any point in the program prior to their usage, most will still be declared at the program's beginning in a single declaration block as was required in ANSI C.

The next block is also indented five spaces and is used for immediate assignments to variables. In this example, strcpy() is used to write a copy of the constant into array *a*. Another blank line separates the initial assignment block from the next program operation.

A *for* loop is presented in the normal fashion. Its single object of control is a call to the cout stream. Note that this line is indented five more spaces. The closing brace signaling termination of the execution run under control of main() is again on the left margin and separated by a blank line. The opening and closing braces encompassing the code under control of main() are easily identified because of their placement in relationship to other program statements.

While the expressiveness of C++ means many things, the presentation of the source code is a major part of it. Let's write the previous program in a most inappropriate manner.

```
#include <iostream.h>
#include <string.h>
int main(){
int x;
```

```
char a[40];
strcpy(a,"Format");
for(x=0;x<=10;++x)
cout << a << endl;}
```

Is this program easy to understand? Of course not. However, it still compiles and executes in exactly the same manner as the previous program did. The compiler sees no difference at all. As a matter of fact, this entire program could have been written on a continuous line with no difference in operation. However, the compiler sees a program in one way and humans see it in another. The example above has no order, it has no expressiveness, and it is, possibly, an over-exaggeration of the way some people are writing C++ source code today.

I came to ANSI C and C++ from a BASIC language environment. One of the major problems with BASIC interpreters of the older genre was the difficulty in easily deciphering its source code, especially when code size ran to several hundred lines. There was little order. With C++ students can comprehend small portions of a complex program. Such a program may initially appear to be extremely simple, especially from the experienced programmer's point of view. However, the student is working in the dark in many areas that are known almost by instinct to the seasoned programmer. The only solution is to have the student break down each program into small blocks. If these blocks are not clearly delineated, the job of learning is increased tremendously.

Proper C++ source code format calls for a space between numeric operators and their left and right values as has been demonstrated throughout this book. Examine the following example.

```
#include <iostream.h>
int main()
{

    int h, i, *x, *y, z;

    i = 10;
    z = 20;

    x = &i;
    y = &z;

    h = *x * *y / (float(*y) / *x);

    cout << h << endl;

}
```

This program is arranged according to good formatting principles. The assignment block has been broken down into three parts. The first assigns auto variables, the second assigns memory addresses to pointers, and the third assigns *h* the value of several mathematical operations on the previous variables. The block could have been written in one section without the blank line separators, but, to me, this would make the program less comprehensible.

Now, let's take this same program and reformat it in the manner some programmers use.

```
#include <iostream.h>
int main()
{
int h,i,*x,*y,z;
i=10;
z=20;
x=&i;
y=&z;
h=*x**y/(float(*y)/*x);
cout << h << endl;
}
```

What we have here is a hodgepodge. The program is so simple that it can be deciphered with a bit of study if you know C ++ fairly well. If not, it may take longer. The point is that the original program (from which this poorly formatted copy was made) is much clearer. The operation of the properly formatted program jumps out at anyone reading the source code who has even a minimal C++ background.

The whitespace between each character in the assignment and declaration lines cleans up the source code. The following line of source code is almost frightening!

```
h = *x**y/(float(*y)/*x);
```

How do we differentiate the multiplicative operator from the indirection operator? They both use the same asterisk symbol (*). Or is *y* in this example a pointer to a pointer using two indirection operators? This program will execute in a normal fashion, but the formatting of the source code is quite corrupt.

GIGO (garbage in, garbage out) is a term coined to describe computer output based on erroneous input. The same applies to a human being. This type of confusing source code format is one of the prime reasons why some programmers have difficulty grasping C++.

Consider the following example, which is even worse.

```
#include <iostream.h>
int main()

{
int h,i,*j,x,*y,**z;
x=14;
y=&x;
z=&y;
i=22;
j=&i;
h=*j***z/**z;
cout << h << endl;
}
```

The assignment to *h* is a killer. What does it mean? Writing it in the following manner answers this question.

```
h = *j * **z / **z;
```

This still wouldn't be an easy expression to decipher, but it would be far simpler.

In order to master C++, you must write your source code in a manner that allows for visual comprehension. A source code format has been established to provide the necessary clarity. It was not arrived at arbitrarily. The conventions used throughout this book have withstood the test of time because they work.

"Why can't I develop my own formatting system that suits me best?" A personal source code format routine seems harmless at first, but in commercial programming environments, others on your team must be able to read what you wrote. If you have your own formatting routine, and ten other team members have theirs, the system breaks down. You may not be working with a team now, but there is always that possibility in the future, so don't develop bad habits.

For me, the correct method of writing C++ source code, from the standpoint of formatting, has become automatic. I do not consider it a shortcut, for instance, to delete the spaces between operators and their left/right values. To delete these spaces purposely would take me far longer than it does to put them in, such is the automatic formatting method that I have embraced during thousands of hours at the keyboard.

You will grasp the concepts of C++ pointers discussed in this book and every other phase of the language if you make yourself adhere to the programming conventions outlined here. However, there are plenty of bad examples of C++ source code around to influence beginners. Unfortunately, many of these less than ideal examples appear in the documentation that accompanies some of the most popular compilers. "If the people who wrote the software do it this way, why shouldn't I?" is a legitimate question that I can only answer with, "Because it's *wrong!*"

C++ Formatting Conventions

The following guidelines originated with pre-ANSI C and have been retained by most C++ programmers. Perhaps they will aid you in formatting your own C++ programs.

Braces

Braces ({}) encompass a major control module. If that module is contained in a function, then the opening brace is positioned on the left margin immediately under the function name, as the example below illustrates.

```
char *strcpy(char *a, char *b)
{
```

When braces are used to confine operational blocks within a program, as would be the case with a loop containing more than one program statement, the opening brace follows the control expression on the same line and is separated by a single whitespace.

```
for (x = 0; x < 456; ++x) {
    cout << x << endl;
    y +=5;
}
```

The closing brace is placed on the margin position that began the control expression and on a separate line immediately beneath the encapsulated statements.

Indentations

Indentations are always made in steps of five. If we assume that main() is located on the left hand margin (indent 0), then all other program statements are indented at locations 5, 10, 15, 20, etc. Assuming the previous *for* loop example begins at indent 5, then the statements within the loop, begin at indent 10. Should there be a nested *for* loop within this one, then the *for* statement would be written at indent 10 and all program statements within this nested loop would be indented another 5 spaces (indent

15). The following program fragment is an example.

```
for (x = 0; x <= 465; ++x) {
        cout << x << endl;
        y += 5;
        for (z = 90; z > 0; -z) {
                strcpy(d, f);
                ++g;
        }
}
```

Note that the closing braces (}) are aligned under the block control elements they terminate. This makes nested operations easier to differentiate.

Parentheses

Parentheses immediately follow a function name but are separated from *for*, *while*, *if* and other statements by a space, as shown below.

```
for (x = 0; x < 5; ++x)
        strcpy(a, b);
```

The *for* statement is separated from the opening paren by a space, whereas the strcpy() function is immediately followed by the paren.

Arithmetic Operators

Arithmetic operators are delineated by a space on the left and on the right. Other types of operators usually are not.

```
i = x + y * z;
```

This statement clearly shows the use of arithmetic operators as opposed to other operator types. The expression below contains other types of operators along with those used for arithmetic purposes.

```
i = x++ + ++y * *z;
```

In this example, the increment operator (++) is not as readily confused with the addition operator(+), and the multiplicative operator(*) is not confused with the indirection operator.

Commas

Commas are always followed by a whitespace when used as argument delineators.

```
add(a, b, c, d, e);
```

The same applies to semicolons used within *for*, *do*, and *while* statements. Note that commas and semicolons are not preceded by a whitespace when used in this manner.

C++ Names and Identifiers

It was an ANSI C tradition to use (with few exceptions) only lower case letters in writing programs. Many reasons were given for this, including the inability of the original MS-DOS linker to differentiate between upper- and lowercase function names. However, the main reason is programming speed, in that it is rarely necessary to press the shift key to access the uppercase alphabet. This does tend to speed things up but sometimes at the cost of program clarity.

At present there is no standard for C++ identifiers. Most C programmers making the switch to C++ continue to program in the familiar lowercase fashion. Those who have entered C++ from other language environments that encourage a mixed-case form of identifier notation will probably carry this style over into C++. For the present, the goal of any programmer should be to write source code that is easy to understand. This is a subjective goal that will be defined in many different ways.

As a rule of thumb, the ANSI C tradition of using uppercase for #define constants will suffice for C++. Most variable names will still be in lowercase, as will function names.

The naming of classes often leans toward a mixed-case format. As an example, an ANSI C struct might be named

```
sort_list_ascending
```

whereas, a C++ class would utilize a mixed-case notation of

```
SortListAscending
```

Here, an uppercase letter is used to begin each field of the class name. Programmers have taken to using this mixed-case format for naming class methods as well.

The exact method for naming identifiers will be largely a matter of programmer preference and will hinge on the language base from which the programmer entered C++. The reader should be aware by now that object-oriented C++ source code quickly takes on very large proportions, much more than an equivalent procedural-based program. Thus, maintaining source code clarity is of paramount importance. This statement does not necessarily address maintaining clarity so that other programmers who read your source code can understand it (although this is a strong consideration where team efforts are involved). It is essential that clarity be maintained so that you will continue to have a handle on what has taken place when writing your own source code. The simple examples used in this book do not adequately emphasize the ease with which a programmer may become lost in his or her own source code. With this in mind, the programmer must establish a set of identifier rules and adhere to them at all times to eliminate many hours of wasted debugging time due.

Summary

The proper formatting of C++ source code is essential to gain a full understanding of the language. The difference between properly and improperly formatted code is like the difference between a neatly typed letter and one written in a messy scrawl.

By observing a few simple formatting rules, all source code will be easier to understand by you and by those who read your code. Of primary importance is the fact that properly formatted programs will be more easily understood by the programmer who inputs the code lines, allowing for quicker debugging of complex program modules and facilitating changes to existing source code.

Epilogue

Pointers address every aspect of the C++ language. Since every program element must be stored somewhere in memory, pointers allow direct access of these objects at their address locations. This book has dissected many standard C++ operations, revealing their hidden pointer operations and defining alternate means of access.

Through pointers, the programmer gains an intimate understanding of how data are stored, aligned, and used within a program. This knowledge allows programmers to design more efficient applications that make use of the full range of tools available in C++. This design efficiency is gained via a *world* picture of the program beginning at the very core of construction, the allocation of storage for program elements.

This enhanced understanding of C++ pointers should aid the programmer in any problem-solving endeavor. By understanding the hidden operations that take place within any code, the programmer is able to take these aspects into consideration and design applications that are elegant and custom tailored to address the task at hand.

Index